Butch Beard's

B A S I C

BASKETBALL

The Complete Player

Butch Beard's

BASIC
BASKETBALL

The Complete Player

BY **BUTCH BEARD,** NEW JERSEY NETS COACH

WITH GLENN POPOWITZ AND DAVID SAMSON

FOREWORD BY JOHN THOMPSON

Michael Kesend Publishing, Ltd.
New York

Photo credits: George Kalinsky: pp. 13, 15, 21, 24, 29, 67, 77, 91, 103, 127, 131; Jerry Wachter/*Sports Illustrated*: pp. 41, 43; Mike Valeri: p. 61; Paul Vanucci: p. 69; courtesy of the University of Louisville Sports Information; pp. 63, 64; from the NBA: Fernando Medina p. 2; Andrew D. Bernstein p. 21; Scott Cunningham p. 41; Barry Gossage p. 67.
Illustrations pp. 109–119 reprinted from *Stretching*, copyright © 1980 by Bob & Jean Anderson. Shelter Publications/Random House. Reprinted by permission.

Cover & book design: Kim Llewellyn
Illustrations: Lisa Amowitz

Library of Congress Cataloging-in-Publication Data

Beard, Butch, 1947–
    Butch Beard's basic basketball

    Includes index.
    1. Basketball. 2. Basketball—Coaching. 3. Basketball—Training.
    I. Popowitz, Glenn, 1967–   . II. Samson, David, 1968–   .III. Title.
    IV. Title: Basic Basketball.
  GV885.B375 1985
  796.32´32   85-18108

ISBN: 0-935576-48-7

Copyright 1995 Butch Beard

Contents

Foreword by John Thompson

Butch Beard has studied the game of basketball from numerous vantages. In college, he was a three time All-American at the University of Louisville. He later became a point guard for several teams on the professional level culminating in a NBA championship with the Golden State Warriors.

He played for and learned from coaches ranging from Al Attles at Golden State to Red Holzman of the New York Knicks and later served under Holzman as an assistant coach. For a time, Butch was a network television basketball analyst covering the NBA. He coached at the college level for three years as head coach at Howard University. Recently, he was named head coach of the New Jersey Nets of the NBA.

In this superb "how-to" book, Butch imparts his knowledge and experience to young developing players—both men and women—and to their coaches.

Butch has a natural feeling and patience for teaching and communicating the fundamentals of the game. All the basics every player needs, from passing to shooting to dribbling are broken down and diagrammed. There are drills and plays, offense and defense that he details in clear, understandable language. Butch also addresses conditioning and the mental aspects of the game.

His book is a thorough and considered overview of basic basketball that any young player and their coach can benefit from. A job well done!

John Thompson
Georgetown University

Acknowledgments

I would like to thank my family for giving me the encouragement to do this book. I would also like to acknowledge my many coaches throughout my career. I know that often they thought I wasn't paying attention to them during those years, so I offer this book as proof that I was listening.

Basketball has also enabled me to make many valuable and close friendships which I am grateful for. You have all helped make me a better person.

And finally, heartfelt thanks to Glenn Popowitz and David Samson, my coauthors, without whom this project never would have gotten started. More than two years ago they convinced me "There's a book in your head!" Since then they have spent countless hours and months extracting the words from me, editing and organizing.

Butch Beard
New York

1

Introduction

Basketball is a game of physical and mental proficiencies, a combination of natural and acquired skills which, when properly and efficiently executed, is like a beautiful blending of sport and ballet. Playing the game well requires endurance, finesse, power, speed, and intensity, along with split-second timing and a fanatical dedication to honing numerous skills. At the high school and college levels, the only way a player can develop these skills is by putting in the hours. That means a commitment to hard work, to practicing year-round, and to finding new ways to improve.

The age-old cliche "Rome was not built in a day" applies equally well to the basketball player. Growth and maturation take time, the amount of which varies from athlete to athlete. If you are a young player, keep in mind that you are changing, both physically and mentally, and that you will not reach your full maturity as a basketball player until you are in your early twenties. Parents and coaches, too: Don't expect that a fourteen-year-old can shoot, pass, or dribble as well as an older player. He can't. But if both the fourteen-year-old *and* the parents and coach recognize the young player's potential, then an atmosphere of encouragement and dedication can be nurtured, and the young player can ultimately flower.

You can't develop as a basketball player—or as anything else, for that matter—without dedication. Dedication is the compass that guides the young player along the road to self-improvement and success. If you feel you are starting to get serious about basketball, ask yourself how good you think you can

be, and then sit down and start developing a plan and an attitude that can help you realize your possibilities. Start thinking about practice, for example, not as drudgery, but as an intensive means to help you develop your basketball fundamentals. Regard drills not as backbreaking labor, but as your allies, there to help you perfect your technique, timing and body control on the court. In short, *start to get yourself motivated.* Once you feel that way, try to hold that motivated feeling in everything you do, both on and off the court.

THE COMPLETE PLAYER

The reason for building this sense of mental fierceness in yourself is not to impress your coach, family, or friends (though you will eventually impress them, believe me), but to help you evolve toward what I like to call "the complete player." Who is he? What is he like?

The complete player is that special athlete who through hard work and dedication "has it all." He is not necessarily a "natural." Yet he has poise, presence and ability which he puts together in a noticeable fashion both on and off the court. As a true leader, he leads by example. He comes to the gym or arena every day, ready to play. He is coachable and enthusiastic and rarely complains. He keeps his teammates loose in the locker room and on the floor during games. He tries to maintain his enthusiasm whether he is playing or sitting on the bench and rooting for his teammates. When things look bad, he

Going for the rebound

is the kind of person who accentuates the positive both to his teammates and his coach. He is intense, calm, and scrappy. He loves the game. He has guts.

One of the most visible traits is his ability to take full advantage of his moments on the court to perfect his game. During workouts and pregame warm-ups, he wastes no time fooling around. Instead, he concentrates on those facets of his game he is not completely satisfied with and continuously strives to improve, he spends countless hours alone in the gym perfecting his game, and there's no such thing as an off-season for him—he practices year-round. In fact, he realizes that most of the significant work done by basketball's greats was done during the off-season. The complete player knows, for example,

that as a boy the brilliant Oscar Robertson used to shoot baskets in his city's park by the moonlight because there were no artificial lights. Robertson's dedication and determination, the complete player realizes, paid off in countless ways in his thirteen years as a pro. The complete player will tell you that during the off-season, Bill Bradley, now a United States senator, used to stack wooden chairs on his high school basketball court to simulate a pick for himself so that he could practice getting a jump shot off in that situation. He did this so often that he developed one of the most accurate and quickly released shots in the game. Darrel Griffith of the Utah Jazz improved his ballhandling skills by using the "Twelve Chairs Drill" which we'll discuss in Chapter

4. He practiced on his own time, at night, in his college's gym. The result is that Griffith is one of the better ballhandlers in the game today. All of these men, the complete player knows, were determined to improve their individual skills and made the most of their time.

For the athlete striving to become the complete player, his all-around game is pursued with an eye toward being the best at everything he does. He plays offense and defense equally well. His ballhandling skills, be they dribbling or passing, are executed with a minimum of turnovers, and his overall timing is crisp and precise. On defense he's a bull. He boxes out the opposition on both offensive and defensive boards, sets picks, challenges the opposition and generally "sees" the court with astonishingly total vision. He is a whirlwind, a dynamo: always a step ahead of everyone else. His teammates look to him in critical situations because they know from his past performances that he always rises to the occasion when called upon.

If the idea of ever being a complete basketball player seems foreign to you, think again: The complete player could be you. Sure, it takes natural ability, and you may never become a Larry Bird or Kareem Abdul-Jabbar; but with practice and dedication you can be a far better player than you are now, and it's the purpose of this book to show you how.

Butch Beard's Basic Basketball: The Complete Player provides *you,* the developing player, and *your coach* with a step-by-step instruction for achieving excellence in basketball. Included in the book are:

- Keys to the fundamentals so that you can learn to shoot, pass, dribble, fake and rebound like the pros

- Sixteen drills for perfecting your all-around game

- Motivational thoughts for boys, girls, men, women—any player at *any* level who wants to play better basketball

- Detailed chapters on time-proven offenses and defenses that can work for you and your team

- Conditioning and stretching exercises that will help you play better and avoid injury both on and off the court

- Handy tips on nutrition, taping and diagnosing the eleven most common basketball injuries

- Five criteria for choosing a summer basketball camp

- A five-day practice guide for player, coach and team

- Ways to improve your mental attitude toward teammates, coach and game

- Valuable insights that will illuminate your basketball understanding whether you're a player, coach, parent or fan

- Goals to shoot for so that *you* can become *a complete player*

I love basketball: its grace, its harmonies, its possibilities. More than anything else, I hope this book helps you love basketball, too.

B.B.
New York City

2

Fundamentals I

SHOOTING

Every sport has its fundamentals. In baseball, these include hitting, running, fielding and throwing; in golf, driving, chipping, and putting; in tennis, serving and hitting (forehand, backhand, and overhand). No player has ever been proficient in any of these sports without first mastering its fundamentals. The same applies in basketball. If you ever hope to become a complete basketball player, you must first master basketball's fundamentals of *shooting, passing, dribbling, faking, and rebounding.* Trust me: There is no way around this hard fact. Fail to hone these five fundamentals, slough off on any one, and you'll find yourself spending more time on the bench, wondering why you're not in the game where you'd like to be.

In the next two chapters, I'm going to take you through those fundamentals, concentrating exclusively in this chapter on shooting. Pay careful attention to the illustrations that accompany the instruction, and start picturing in your mind *you* executing the maneuvers well. This process of *imaging*—that is, visualizing yourself taking a shot, etc.—is quickly becoming a proven way to prepare an athlete's mind and body for successful play.

SHOOTING

Many young players in the heat of play forget that the object of basketball is to score. No amount of fancy dribbling or passing will help a team if its players can't put the ball through the hoop. In fact, if it hasn't already occurred to you, start thinking of passing and dribbling merely as a means to an end: the creation of scoring opportunities. No higher premium should be placed on any phase of your game than shooting and scoring.

Of course, shooting is something you can do from virtually anywhere on the court. That means you've got to develop a variety of shots suitable for any scoring opportunity. In addition, if you're not doing so already, *you must start learning to shoot with either hand.* Few players, even the great ones, are ambidextrous; but with practice, you can start sinking shots with your "weak" hand. Also, start learning to go to your left and right on a shot, especially lay-ups, so that you are equally effective shooting from either direction (and so that your opponent does not scout you as a player who can go only to his left or right!).

There are ten basic shots in basketball:

- *the one-handed jump shot*

- *the fall-away jump shot*

- *the bank shot*

- *the hook shot*

- *the lay-up*

- *the over-the-rim lay-up*

- *the driving hook lay-up*

- *the dunk*

- *the tip*

- *the foul shot*

Let's look at each, with an emphasis on the keys to making the shot go in.

The One-Handed Jump Shot

It's hard to believe that the jump shot didn't always exist. Forty years ago, the only long shot that players took was the set shot, performed usually by pushing the ball with two hands from the chest to the basket, much like a two-handed push pass.

Then it was discovered that if you jumped first and released the shot at the top of the jump, you greatly improved your chances of getting the shot over your opponent without it being blocked and thus elevated your scoring percentage dramatically.

Today, the one-handed jump shot is the most used outside shot in the game. Without it in your arsenal, you concede at least half your offensive game.

Shooting the One-Handed Jump Shot. In shooting the one-handed jump shot, always control the ball with the fingertips, and not the palms of the hands. Hold the ball with the long seams parallel to the floor (known as seams up), the left hand gripping the lower half, the right hand cradling the ball from behind, along the seams. While holding the ball this way, bend your knees slightly and stand in a semi-crouch position, ready to jump.

Now move the ball up from in front of your chest to a point just above eye level, and as you do, spring up off your toes and jump. Be prepared to experiment with just how high you want to hold the ball for the jump and subsequent release. Some players release the ball just above eye level; others prefer extending their arms and shooting the ball well above the head. Find the ball position that works best for you and stick with it.

At the peak of the jump as your arms start to extend, let go of the ball with the left hand and continue to push the ball up and forward with the right. As you do, you should be able to look up along the length of your extending right arm and sight the front edge of the basket. That is your target, and with

Extension on the jump shot

The Jump Shot

Always keep your eyes on the front lip of the rim

practice, you should be able to drop your shots over that lip and through the net for a score. The important thing is to *keep your eye on that front lip.* By doing so, your follow-through will be correct: your right arm will extend fully, your wrist will snap backward and down, the fingers of your right hand will impart the necessary backspin on the ball, and the ball itself will arc in a perfect trajectory toward its goal.

Many young players learning the jump shot make the mistake of starting the shot with the right elbow sticking out away from the body. The result is a weak, inaccurate shot, though a pretty good imitation of a flapping chicken. Instead of making this mistake, try, as you start your cradling and jumping motions for the shot, to keep your right elbow tucked in as close to the body as you can. The result is a more efficient total motion and a higher percentage of buckets.

To hit your jump shot with any consistency, you must be comfortable and relaxed. Don't bother trying to copy another player's shooting form; every player is different. If you try to copy the moves of a 6'8" player when you're only 5'9", you're more than likely going to develop bad shooting habits, which, when ingrained in your mind, will be tough to unlearn. Remember the keys discussed above, and stick with what's comfortable for you.

The same rule of individuality applies to the arc of your jump shot. Arc is a product of jumping form and follow-through. If your jump shot travels in a fairly flat arc and yet you can still sink the shot nine times out of ten, why mess with that statistic by trying to shoot rainbows? On the other hand, if you can't make the shot with accuracy, maybe it's time to go back to basics and start reworking your grip, extension, jump, and follow-through.

(Incidentally, for you lefties reading these instructions, the proper motion is a mirror image of that for the right-hander. That is, where I say right, think left; where I say left, think right.)

The Fall-Away Jump Shot

The fall-away jump shot is one of the most beautiful to behold in basketball—unless, of course, you happen to be guarding the fall-away shooter! It enables a player to free himself from a tightly guarded situation and still score two points. The technique used in releasing the ball—the arm extension, wrist action, and follow-through—are exactly the same as with the regular jump shot. Only the jumping movement is different.

Shooting the Fall-Away Jump Shot. To perform a fall-away jump shot as you would in a game situation, imagine yourself pivoting away from both the defensive man and the goal (this is usually how most fall-away jump shots begin). Follow this pivoting movement with a high, backward jump—*don't jump straight up!* At the top of the jump, make your shot. Your momentum upward and backward on the jump will cause you to land several feet farther away from your opponent than where you started. You should experiment with your fall-away jump shot. Oftentimes, because of the backward movement involved in the shot and the angle at which they're shooting, players find they have better luck banking the shot off the backboard. But see what works best for you. There are players who can shoot the fall-away jumper over the rim with just as deadly accuracy as their regular jump shot.

The Bank Shot

The bank shot is a form of the jump shot normally most successful when taken in the area just outside the foul lanes and between the first two rebounders' marks.

Shooting the Bank Shot. To shoot a bank shot, position yourself six to eight feet from the basket at an angle and, concentrating on the small square on the backboard, take a regular jump shot, making sure to release the ball softly at the top of the jump, and follow through with the proper arm and wrist motion. The ball should hit the backboard within the square, and, if you've used the correct touch and avoided putting any English on the ball, it should drop through the goal with or without hitting the rim.

Many times the bank shot is effective in traffic, particularly when used in connection with some sort of fake and fall-away jumping motion. It can also be used when a defenseman is otherwise in position to block your drive to the basket; simply stop fast, jump straight up and bank your shot off the glass before the defenseman can adjust.

The bank shot has further value on the fast break and during the transition game because the back-

The Hook Shot

Release the ball softly

board softens your shots even when the momentum of your body has you leaning forward or out of control.

Once you become proficient at the bank shot at close range, you'll find it can be effective when shooting from the wings at distances of up to fifteen feet. Whatever the distance you shoot the bank shot from, you should know exactly where you are on the floor and should concentrate on the square behind the goal throughout the entire shot.

The bank shot is sometimes scoffed at by finesse players, yet the player who can shoot one accurately becomes a greater scoring threat.

The Hook Shot

The hook shot has tremendous value, yet many players never develop it. They should, though. A center can use the hook shot in numerous situations, and forwards, too, can find instances to use it to their advantage. In fact, the hook shot can be very helpful to any player who likes to post low (that is, play down near the basket) on an offensive pattern. One only has to look at pictures of Kareem Abdul-Jabbar performing his patented "sky hook" to see just how effective the hook shot can be. Kareem makes the hook look so easy that it appears easier to shoot than a jump shot. It isn't; but with practice you can make the hook shot look easy, too.

Shooting the Hook Shot. To shoot the hook shot, start by taking a position approximately three to five feet from the goal and at an angle so you can bank the ball off the backboard. Now imagine a line of the floor running outward from a point under the basket to where you are standing. Position your feet so that you are standing on this imaginary line and your right arm is the farthest from the basket. Now hold the ball on the fingertips of your right hand, with the rest of your hand underneath the ball. After extending your right arm so that it is parallel to the floor, start it upward toward the backboard (or, if you prefer, the basket). As you do so, raise your right knee until the upper leg is parallel to the floor and your left forearm so that it forms a right angle with your upper arm and is parallel to your chest (the left arm serves as a stabilizer and is used to keep the defender away from the ball) and rise up on the toes of your left foot. You should sight the backboard or front rim of the basket (depending on whether or not you intend to bank the shot) over your left shoulder, and the motion of your right arm should be smooth and fluid, the elbow semi-locked the entire way. At the moment the right arm reaches the vertical position, release the ball with the fingertips, snapping the wrist down as the ball spins free.

Your first few attempts at a hook shot may produce disastrous hard line-drives at the basket. Don't despair if your shots are too hard. Experiment with the amount of "touch" or softness you need to impart on the ball in order to give it the right amount of arc and backspin. You'll soon find that all the speed and control in releasing the shot comes at the last moment from the wrist and fingertips; the arm merely raises the ball into position for the launch. You'll also notice that your body position and the angle of the shot are determined by where you are relative to the basket.

A useful drill when learning the hook shot is to position yourself three to five feet from the goal and at an angle to it so you can use the backboard. Make a hook shot with your right hand. Take the ball out of the net, pivot (possibly dribbling once), and in the same rhythm and motion take a hook shot with your left hand. Repeat this procedure using your right hand. Then left again, and so on. When shooting with the left hand, be sure to rise off your right foot; when shooting with the right hand, vice versa. Practice taking the ball out of the net and alternating with the right and left hands until you are hitting the hook shot either way with great accuracy.

The hook shot is difficult to perfect but the time it takes to improve it is well spent. The hook shot is almost impossible to block without fouling the shooter and can result in three-point plays (two points for scoring the field goal and one point for the foul shot).

The Lay-Up

Being able to shoot a lay-up proficiently is an absolute must for any player no matter what position he plays; forward, guard or center. Many young players find it difficult to shoot a lay-up with their "weak" hand. If you're one of them, make it a point to try to correct this deficiency. Don't assume that the shot will develop by itself—it won't. Perfecting the lay-up takes a great deal of practice. Yet to be a complete

The lay-up

The Lay-Up

Release the ball at the top of the jump

player, you absolutely *must* be able to shoot a lay-up from either side of the basket and equally well with either hand. Furthermore, as a complete player, you should be confident you can sink the lay-up every time you shoot one.

There are actually several different kinds of lay-ups. Each is a variation of what I call the *regular lay-up.*

The Regular Lay-Up. The regular lay-up is most often used on a running drive from the right or left and toward the basket. Shooting it properly requires that you be relaxed and that you concentrate on banking the ball off the backboard and into the goal. You should use the backboard whenever possible because it will absorb the impact of the ball and will direct the ball into the basket regardless of whether the shot is too hard or too soft.

What part of the backboard should you aim for? The precise answer depends on the angle at which you approach the basket. *Generally, you should concentrate on banking the ball within the area of the square box outlined on the backboard just above the goal.* For an added measure of accuracy, think of your approach to the basket as a kind of high jump rather than a broad jump.

Shooting the Regular Lay-Up. To shoot a regular right-handed lay-up, start back twelve to fifteen feet and at an angle to the right of the basket and dribble the ball, starting forward on your right foot. Next, jump up off your left foot and extend the ball in your right hand as high as you can. At the top of your jump, release the ball so that it hits the backboard within the area of the painted square as gently as possible. To repeat: *where the ball should hit the backboard is determined by the angle of the shot.* Try to control the ball with your fingertips, giving it minimal spin. A ball with lots of spin must be shot extremely accurately, or the ball will glance off the rim and spin out.

I can't stress enough the importance of trying to high jump rather than broad jump (jumping forward) when shooting a lay-up. If you start your jump too soon, you won't be able to concentrate well on the backboard as you approach it, and your forward momentum will make getting off a soft shot very difficult.

To shoot a lay-up from the left side of the goal,

jump off your right foot and bank the ball gently off the backboard using the fingertips of your left hand.

The Reverse Lay-Up. This particular lay-up is used when making a baseline move with the ball (a move underneath the basket, from one side to the other). When executed properly, it puts the hoop between the shooter and the defenseman, and the hoop actually prevents the defensive man from making a good defensive play. These shots are most often taken by forwards and centers, since those players traditionally operate close to the goal, but coaches would be well advised to teach their guards this particular move which would add an element of surprise to their offensive attack.

Shooting the Reverse Lay-Up. To shoot a reverse lay-up, be relaxed and concentrate your attention on the backboard. You will start your jump on one side of the basket but end up taking your shot on the other side.

Let's say you're dribbling the ball across the baseline from right to left. At the moment you are under and to the right of the basket, jump off your right foot, this time *broad jumping instead of high jumping* (this is one time when broad jumping will help you get the shot off). Your object is to gain as much height as possible, while also going for horizontal distance. If you jump correctly (and you should practice the jump many times with and without the ball to get it down pat), you should feel as if you are floating underneath the basket. As you make your float, switch the ball from your right to your left hand, lift it as high as you can, and twisting your left hand at an angle toward the goal, bank the ball off the backboard in exactly the same spot that you aim for when shooting a regular lay-up. If you're a young player, this shot may be extremely difficult for you—you may have to practice the jump and the ball transfer many times before they feel comfortable to you. But if you concentrate on the backboard as you float past it during your jump, the knack for making the shot will eventually come to you. Try to avoid putting a lot of spin, or English, on the ball when you shoot it. When crossing from left to right beneath the basket, jump off your left foot and transfer the ball from your left hand to your right.

You'll know you've mastered the reverse lay-up when you can shoot it at will with either hand. It's a terrific shot to have under your belt when the basket area is congested, and I urge you to perfect it, no matter what position you play.

The Over-the-Rim Lay-Up. This lay-up is difficult to master and should not be shot when a regular lay-up is possible. It is, however, frequently used on a three-man fast break when the man in the middle takes the shot. What makes it so difficult? First, you aren't using the backboard to soften the shot; the ball rolls right over the rim. Second, many players take the shot using a fingertip roll, palm upward, which is a tricky release to control. Third, try as they might otherwise, most players have a tendency to broad jump on their approach for this shot, and thus carry too much momentum to control the ball's release (there are exceptions, of course; most notably Julius Erving, whose great athletic ability makes his approach look easy). Despite its dangers, the over-the-rim lay-up is a useful shot, one not to be neglected by the complete player.

Shooting the Over-the-Rim Lay-Up. The principles of shooting the over-the-rim lay-up are the same as for the regular lay-up.

When shooting this lay-up right-handed, jump off the left foot as high as possible and release the ball off the fingertips of the right hand with the palm facing up. You'll see that the upward angle of the palm allows the ball to roll softly off the fingertips, causing it to spin only slightly.

When shooting a left-handed over-the-rim lay-up, jump off your right foot, and release the ball from your left hand in the same manner as with the right.

Concentrate on the front edge of the rim when making this shot! You can bank the ball off the backboard, but if you do, you must shoot the ball without English in the square over the hoop in order for it to go in.

The Driving-Hook Lay-Up. This shot is used mostly on fast breaks by guards when they are in heavy traffic and a regular lay-up might be blocked, or when the forwards or center receive the ball at the foul line and feel they can drive with it to the hoop. It's a shot whose chances of going in are definitely improved by using the backboard and which requires the shooter to jump up (high jump) rather than forward (broad jump) while protecting the ball before the release.

Shooting the Driving-Hook Lay-Up. To shoot a driving-hook lay-up, you must remember to high jump and concentrate on banking the ball within the area of the square on the backboard. The purpose of aiming for that target is simple: If you shoot the ball too hard, or if your forward momentum carries your body out of control, the backboard will soften the shot.

The actual shooting motion for a right-handed driving hook is the same as for a regular right-handed hook shot; that is, as you make your drive toward the basket, jump off your left foot, turn so that your right arm is farthest from the basket, and raise your right hand, which cradles the ball from underneath, in the hooking motion. While your left arm serves as a bumper/stabilizer, your right hand rises until it reaches the vertical position, whereupon you release the ball with a downward snap of your fingertips and wrist.

The key to an accurate driving-hook lay-up with either hand is to turn your head as you start your jump so that you can concentrate on the spot behind the hoop where you want to place the ball.

The Dunk

The dunk is the most electrifying shot in basketball. It can intimidate the opposition, boost the scoring team's morale, and change the tempo of a game in a split second. Coaches in the college and pro ranks like to see their big men dunk, not only for the psychological boost it gives the team, but also because the dunk is commonly considered the 100 percent successful shot. Naturally, every player on the court likes to be known as a dunker; unfortunately, it's not an easy shot to perform unless you are tall enough and your legs are strong enough to make the shot. If you're in junior high or high school and can't dunk yet, but have good jumping ability, be patient: it will come.

There are a variety of dunk shots ranging from the basic one-hander to the two-handed over-the-head dunk. Regardless of which type of dunk you attempt, the most important keys to remember are 1) jumping high, and 2) turning the wrist over properly when the hand is above the rim.

Shooting the Dunk. To shoot a dunk in a break-away situation, apply the same principles you followed when you shot a regular lay-up. Jump *up,* not forward (high jump, don't broad jump), jumping high enough so that your hand (or hands if you're shooting a two-handed dunk) clears the rim by at least five inches. At the top of your jump, release the ball into the goal with a sharp downward flick of the wrist (or wrists). If you have cleared the rim by five inches, you should have no difficulty with the downward wrist flick. Usually, it's when players fail to jump high enough that their dunks ricochet wildly off the rim and miss.

Just as you did for the regular lay-up, learn to shoot the breakaway dunk by jumping off of one foot. By doing so, you prevent the defense from gaining a split second that you otherwise give them if you pause to set and jump from two feet.

To shoot the dunk shot after grabbing an offensive rebound, you must, of course, jump from two feet. Gather yourself after grabbing the rebound, plant your feet about a shoulder's width apart, bend your knees slightly, push off on both feet and go up for the dunk. You must go up strongly and quickly because in a game situation the defense will be trying either to block your shot or foul you. A quick, strong jump means everything.

If you are a big, strong player you should dunk every chance you get, especially when you are within five feet of the basket. Whatever you do, however, don't take your dunk shot for granted. Practice it. The dunk may seem easy to you, but in fact it requires precise timing and controlled jumping ability for it to go in 100 percent of the time.

The Tip

The tip is another heavy-traffic shot taken close to the boards, usually by centers and forwards. Still, guards can profit, too, from learning the tip. It can be used to great advantage 1) when play is crowded under the boards, 2) when the ball is in the air, 3) to keep the ball alive so it can be tipped a second time for two points, 4) when a player can't get off any other shot.

Shooting the Tip Shot. To shoot a tip, stand close to the basket, holding the ball in the fingertips of both hands and jump straight up, extending the ball in

Going strong to the hoop

your hands as high as you can. At the top of the jump, gently push the ball over the rim with your right hand, controlling the ball's path with fingertip and arm action. Do not slap the ball over the rim; control it with a soft wrist flick. The most important facet of the shot is the release at the top of the jump. Don't hesitate to use the backboard if you have the proper angle, and learn to time your movements so that you can make a second jump and tip if the ball doesn't go in the first time.

Practicing tips by gently bouncing the ball off the backboard in repetitions of five to ten at a time is a great way to develop both the dexterity and soft hands for the shot, and the tip itself is one of those small but effective weapons that can help you toward your goal of becoming a complete player.

The Foul Shot

How many times have you seen or played in a basketball game that was won or lost on the foul line? Probably more times than you can remember. And yet there are players even in the pros who never develop a consistent, reliable foul shot. What a waste! A foul shot is literally a "free throw"; the opposition, by fouling a player, has in effect, handed him the opportunity to score another point or pair of points. How foolish, then, to blow that opportunity by taking a ragged, inconsistent shot! There is no excuse for an otherwise competent player to make less than 65 percent of his foul shots. Seventy to 75 percent is considered average in the college and pro ranks. If you're aspiring to be a complete basketball player, a better than 75 percent average at the foul line should be your minimal goal.

Shooting the Foul Shot. The foul shot is really the one shot in basketball where each player can and should develop his own style. Most players shoot a variation of the one-handed set shot, whose mechanics are exactly like those of the one-handed jump shot, minus the jump. A few players still shoot the between-the-legs underhand foul shot, and I recommend it to very young players who may not have the strength to shoot an overhand shot. Whatever shooting technique you use, though, you should always try to relax yourself on the line (by exhaling hard as you take your position, shaking out your hands, arms, and legs), and then concentrating on the mechanics of shooting the ball. After a while, you'll develop a certain rhythm and routine at the line that makes you comfortable; once you've got that routine down, and you're sinking your foul shots with a certain regularity, stick to it. The foul line is the place for little rituals.

Many young players wonder what part of the basket or backboard they should focus on while shooting a foul shot. The answer is, the same part of the basket you focus on when shooting any other shot around the key: the front rim. Look at the front rim during every phase of your foul shot, from the time you position yourself on the line, to when you raise the ball and actually shoot. Never, ever, follow the flight of the ball to the basket. Watch only the rim. Your object, as with any shot, is to drop the ball over the rim and into the basket for the score. By taking your eyes off the rim as you launch the ball, you risk misdirecting the shot.

Many players are unconscious of taking their eyes off the rim as they shoot a foul shot. To make sure that you're not guilty of this error, have a teammate station himself along either of the foul lanes as you practice your foul shots and ask him to watch your eyes. If you're concentrating on the rim, your eyes should not move during any phase of the shot.

I played with probably the best free-throw shooter in the history of modern basketball, Rick Barry. Interestingly, Rick believed—and I agree with him—that if you have your rhythm, routine, and mechanics for the foul shot down pat, you should be able to make seven out of ten shots with your eyes closed. Try it the next time you practice. The results could be very revealing!

Two things more: Somewhere during the course of every day's practice, you should make a point of shooting, at minimum, a hundred foul shots in a row. That doesn't mean you have to *make* every shot (though it's certainly a goal to try for); but such a routine is the only way you'll become a better foul shooter.

Second, never, ever forget that the foul shot is a gift. Use it to your advantage and treat it with the importance it deserves.

The Foul Shot

(A) The set   **(B) The bend**   **(C) The follow-through**

IMPORTANT REMINDERS FOR BECOMING A BETTER SHOOTER

1. *Be relaxed and concentrate on the basket.* Again, your focus of attention should be on that part of the rim nearest you as you shoot. The only exceptions are the bank shot and the lay-up where you should concentrate on that part of the backboard where you will bank the ball.

2. *Develop the ability to know when you have a good shot and take it.* Don't develop a reputation as the team "gunner"; but still, if you think you can make a shot, go for it. There is such a thing as being too unselfish on the court, particularly when you're new to the game.

3. *On the jump shot, take a nice natural jump—don't force it.* Concentrate on jumping straight up and releasing the shot at the peak of the jump, in one fluid, continuous motion.

4. *Be balanced when you shoot your jump shot, or any other shot.*

5. *Make sure you use the proper shooting mechanics.*

6. *Follow through on every shot.*

7. *Put an arc on every shot.* Remember, so long as the ball goes through the hoop, the degree of arc is a matter of personal preference.

8. *When shooting free-throws, be relaxed, keep your knees slightly bent.*

9. *When shooting free-throws, avoid excess motion.* Use only the motion needed to make the shot.

10. *Practice all your shots.* You can't practice shooting enough! (Practice, practice, practice, practice, practice . . .)

3

Fundamentals II

PASSING
DRIBBLING
FAKES
REBOUNDING

PASSING

Other than scoring, passing is the most essential fundamental in basketball. Without good passing, a team is literally without an offense, since so much of offensive play hinges on precise ball movement from player to player.

A good passer is one who is unselfish and who really wants to pass the ball to someone else. In fact, good passing is contagious; one good passer can infect an entire team. When that happens, the team improves dramatically. Suddenly, it can advance the ball with ease, pass to the open man, cope with difficult defenses, and make its offensive plays work.

In today's pro game, two superstars, Larry Bird of the Boston Celtics and Magic Johnson of the Los Angeles Lakers, pass so well that they not only make their team and teammates look better, they also elevate the entire level of play.

There are three keys to becoming an excellent passer:

1. *All passes are controlled by the fingertips.* There is never a time when you should handle the ball with your palms.

2. *Good wrist action is essential.* Be aware of your wrists as you practice passing.

3. *Good follow-through is a must.* There is a tendency among players at any level to neglect this phase, but without follow-through, the pass will be weak and often inaccurate.

As you progress in passing, you'll discover that the type of pass you use, as well as its arc, speed, and height, is determined by the defensive situation. You'll learn to use your peripheral vision so that you don't have to look at the man to whom you're passing, and thus aren't "telegraphing" your intentions to the defense. You'll learn a variety of head, hand, and body fakes in order to get the pass away cleanly; and you'll learn teamwork and timing, particularly on lead passes and fast breaks.

There are twelve passes in basketball:

- *the two-handed chest pass*
- *the two-handed bounce pass*
- *the two-handed underhand pass*
- *the one-handed underhand pass*
- *the two-handed overhead pass*
- *the baseball or long pass*
- *the hook pass*
- *the jump pass*
- *the roll pass*
- *the tap pass*
- *the lob pass*
- *the off-the-dribble pass*

To be a complete player, you must be proficient in all of them. Knowing both *how* to make the passes and *when* to use them in a game situation are the hallmarks of a successful passer.

The Two-Handed Chest Pass

The two-handed chest pass is probably the most used pass in basketball. It is basic to any style of play and is usually used in short-distance situations.

To make a two-handed chest pass, spread your fingertips wide and grasp the ball on either side, slightly above its midline, being sure that the ball rests on your fingertips and not in your palms.

Bring the ball to your chest. Your elbows should be slightly out from your sides and your wrists fairly loose as you start to extend your arms forward. As your arms approach full extension, release the ball from your fingertips by snapping your wrists both forward and up. This wrist snap is an indication of proper follow-through and also puts backspin on the ball, which makes the ball easier for a receiver to catch and control.

NOTE: You don't have to step in the direction of your pass, but it will improve your passing accuracy and thus you should try to do so when first learning the pass. Stepping also puts more force on the ball and thus is a must when making a long pass.

The Two-Handed Bounce Pass

The two-handed bounce pass is often an effective way to get the ball to your teammate on the high or low post areas. Its biggest drawback is that it's the slowest pass in basketball and thus susceptible to being picked off by the defense. When making this pass, normally your teammate will have broken away from the defense; nonetheless, the timing of the pass is critical.

When making a two-handed bounce pass, you apply many of the same techniques used for the two-handed chest pass. The only difference is that now you are passing the ball on a single bounce and therefore you must consider both the spot on the floor where the ball will hit and the location of your receiver.

Again, start by grasping the ball on each side in your fingertips, with your fingers spread wide and your hands a little above the ball's midline. Next, bring the ball to the level of your chest, keeping your elbows slightly out from your sides and your wrists loose and flexible, and extend your arms forward and down, aiming the ball toward the spot where

The Two-Handed Chest Pass

Be sure the ball rests on your fingertips

you want it to bounce. Where should that spot be?

The angle and amount of force you use will determine both the ball's bounce spot and its final destination. Ideally, when releasing the ball, you want it to bounce on the floor so that it reaches the receiver about waist high. There are times when this pass can be received a little below the waist, but never below the knees.

As with the two-handed chest pass, wrist snap is critical when making a two-handed bounce pass. Proper wrist snap ensures both good follow-through and backspin, vital ingredients to accuracy and control.

The Two-Handed Bounce Pass

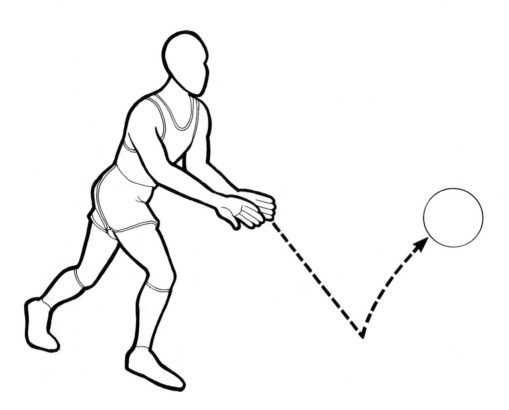

To insure proper follow through hands should be turned outwards after the pass is thrown

The Two-Handed Underhand Pass

The two-handed underhand pass is also known as the shovel pass. Although not used a great deal, it does have its uses, particularly when the passer is tightly guarded.

When making a two-handed shovel pass, 1) move your hands from the sides to the lower half of the ball, keeping the ball in your fingertips, 2) pivot *away* from the defenseman and flip the ball in an underhand motion, aiming at the receiver's waist. Keep the wrists locked throughout the motion and follow through with only the arms. The key to the success of this pass is the follow-through.

Most often the two-handed underhand pass is made at distances of six to ten feet when the receiver is almost parallel to the passer. Thus, it's a handy feed to use when a teammate is clear for a drive toward the basket.

The One-Handed Underhand Pass

The one-handed underhand pass is used much more than the two-handed version because it's quicker to execute and far more accurate and reliable. Guards use it as an outlet pass to start a fast break, usually passing over a distance of six to twelve feet, while centers like to use it in congested areas as a shorter two to three foot feed pass to a teammate cutting toward the basket.

When making a one-handed underhand pass, cup the underside of the ball in your fingertips, draw your hand back to waist level, and swing the arm forward, using a sort of sweeping sidearm hooking motion. As the ball is released, the wrist should snap up and the arm should follow through in an upward arc. Both the wrist snap and follow-through give the pass its necessary speed and spin.

The Two-Handed Overhead Pass

The two-handed overhead pass has traditionally been used as a lead pass for a fast break, but more and more it's gaining a reputation as a big man's pass, used by taller players to break defensive pressure. Centers and big forwards use it particularly against full court zone defenses; because of their size and strength, they can pinpoint the pass over great distances.

In making the two-handed overhead pass, start by holding the side of the ball in both hands, spreading the fingers as wide as possible but in a comfortable position. Next, extend the arms over the head and pass the ball by swinging the arms forward. At the moment of release, snap the wrists down to put speed on the pass, which should be aimed toward the receiver's chest.

If you have to jump off the floor while making this pass, be sure to jump straight up and down. Never jump forward or lean as you descend because in both cases you give the defensive man the chance to draw a charging foul on you by moving under you as you jump.

The Two-Handed Overhead Pass

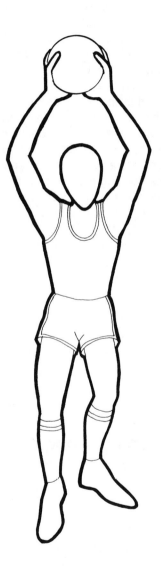

Snap the wrists at the moment of release

The Baseball or Long Pass

The most important thing to remember about the baseball pass is that *it is not a lob;* it is *a straight-line pass* without a high trajectory. You can use it to make an outlet pass to start a fast break, to hit a teammate who is free at the other end of the court, or to move the ball quickly out of traffic under the boards. It's an excellent pass to use after getting a defensive rebound because the movement is so quick and you don't have to bring the ball down where it can be stolen or tied up.

In making a right-handed baseball pass, start by holding the ball in the middle, slightly above the midline, and draw the ball back until it is behind the right ear. The motion is similar to that of a baseball catcher cocking his arm to throw to second base; in each case the cocking motion determines both the speed and accuracy of the throw.

Once the ball is cocked back, throw the ball using a straight overhand motion and aiming your arm, hand, and fingertips toward the intended receiver. As you follow through, your arm should extend fully forward and you should finish the pass with a strong downward snap of the wrist.

Many young players make the mistake of not throwing the baseball pass with an overhand motion. Instead, they jerk the arm back as if they're holding a javelin and throw the ball with a big roundhousing motion. The result is a giant curveball with enough English on it to make it impossible to handle—if it reaches the intended receiver at all! Small-handed players who have difficulty controlling the ball with one hand aren't the only offenders; by palming the ball, big-handed players throw the roundhouse, too. Remember to keep the cocking motion succinct; take the ball just behind an ear—no farther. Then throw the ball forward with a straight overhand motion.

The Baseball or Long Pass

Throw the ball with an overhand motion

The Hook Pass

Like the two-handed overhand pass, the hook pass is most often used by taller players to relieve pressure on themselves when they're tightly guarded by a smaller opponent or opponents; yet other players can make excellent use of it, too. For example, it's a fine pass when your team is trying to stall or freeze out the clock, and many players use it for hitting the open man downcourt, or as an outlet pass to the side to start the fast break.

To make a hook pass, start by holding the underside of the ball in your outstretched fingertips and extending your arm all the way behind you. Your throw should come straight over the top toward the receiver with your elbow kept locked the entire way. The release comes as the ball moves just forward of your head, and you should complete the release with your wrist snapping forward and down. With practice, you'll discover that you can control the speed of your hook passes by the degree of wrist snap you use.

The Jump Pass

The jump pass is a situation pass not used that often in a basketball game, but worth knowing how to make nonetheless. Most often you'll see it used for starting a fast break, or for making a long pass over the head of a defender during a full-court press.

To make one, hold the ball just below the midline in your outstretched fingertips and draw your arm back as far to the right as you can (if you're left-handed, draw your arm back to the left). As you draw your arm back, jump straight up, and at the top of the jump, sling the ball forward using a three quarters overhand motion. Your arm should remain straight throughout the throw and you should complete the motion with a sharp downward snap of the wrist.

The Roll Pass

In game situations, the roll pass is normally used toward the end of a quarter or half to save time on the clock after a dead ball violation.

Remember, the clock does not start until the ball is touched, so if the defense backs off and does not apply pressure, simply roll the ball down the court

The Hook Pass

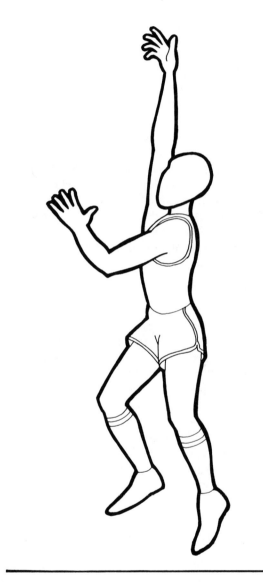

Keep your elbow locked

until the defense forces you or a teammate to pick it up. Be careful, though! When making the roll pass you must keep an eye on the defense, and when rolling the ball inbounds, you must not let it touch the out-of-bounds lines. To do so is equivalent to stepping inbounds before making an inbounds pass and results in a turnover.

The Tap Pass

Since the tap pass involves nothing more than tipping the ball to an open teammate, there is no particular form to follow. You'll find it a handy pass, however, particularly in two-on-one fast break situations when the defender commits to trying to steal the ball away from you as you receive a pass. When that happens, all you do is tap the ball back to the passer who is now free to move for the score.

The tap pass can also be used in a jump ball situation, either to tap the ball backward or forward to the center or to another open man.

The Lob Pass

The lob pass, also known as the "alley oop," is yet another situation pass gaining wide respectability in basketball today. It works well in a fast break leading to an offensive play, but it requires pinpoint timing and is difficult to execute well when on the move.

The mechanics of the pass are exactly the same as for the two-handed overhead pass except that you add a little more arc to it. Another, slightly more reliable, method for making the pass is to push it in a long arc with two hands from waist level.

Again, there are many difficulties to making a good lob pass on the run. And yet it is an excellent pass to make to players who like to post low.

The Off-the-Dribble Pass

The off-the-dribble pass is being used more and more in basketball, and you and every player on your team can profit from knowing it. You can make it in any direction and even bounce it off the floor if you wish. It's especially valuable to guards since their position requires so much dribbling.

The pass is made in the midst of dribbling the ball by quickly moving the dribbling hand from the top of the ball to the top back quarter. Instead of pushing the ball back down to the floor, push it forward. Combine a lateral movement of the hand and arm with a *quick flick of the wrist* to pass the ball to the receiver.

The advantage of the off-the-dribble pass is its quickness. Many times the ball is on its way before the defenseman realizes what's happened, and, because there is no hint of the pass, the defense as a whole doesn't have time to react to it.

Receiving the Pass

No matter how well a pass is thrown, if the receiver doesn't catch it, it's unsuccessful.

The way the ball is caught depends in large measure on the type of pass being made and the position of the defense. Still, regardless of these factors, all passes above the waist should be caught with *fingers up;* all passes below the waist should be caught with *fingers down.*

There are three other factors to remember when receiving a pass:

1. *Always control the ball with the fingertips.* Never catch a ball with your palms. Use your fingers as a spring or cushion to "give" with the ball as it arrives. To develop "soft hands," keep your fingers spread and relaxed, and when receiving a pass, "look" the ball into your fingertips rather than grabbing at it. By being relaxed and catching the ball naturally with spread fingers, you decrease the risk of a fumble and a turnover.

2. *Move toward the ball as it comes to you.* It's discouraging to the passer who makes an excellent pass and harmful to your team's prospects of winning if you receive a pass flat-footed. Nine times out of ten, the defensive man guarding you will steal the ball. Why make his job so easy? By moving toward the ball, you decrease that risk dramatically, and your team's passing game stays alive. The number of steps you should take toward the pass depends on the situation. If the pass is short and quick, one step may be all you can take before the ball is in your hands. However, on longer passes, your position relative to the defense, as well as the type and speed of the pass, will all determine whether or not you should take more steps.

Obviously, the only times you don't move to the

ball are when you are cutting to the hoop or making an adjustment to catch the ball.

3. *Once you receive the ball, always protect it from the defense.* How vigorously you must protect the ball depends upon a) where you receive it: high, low, or wide, b) how the defense is playing you and the size of the defensive man covering you, c) your position on the floor. While protecting the ball, you should try to face the hoop and the defense whenever possible. Always try to keep the ball moving by pivoting, faking, passing, shooting, or dribbling. Never stop the ball. That stops the game, which is built on the movement.

DRIBBLING

Dribbling is the art of bouncing the ball on the floor, and it has so many uses, can control a game's tempo so commandingly, that one of your goals as a budding complete player should be to become an expert dribbler. Once you know its fundamentals, you'll be able to use dribbling 1) to enhance your passing and shooting skills, 2) to penetrate the other team's defense more effectively, 3) to set up your offensive players in the positions you want them, 4) to take advantage of fast breaks.

Younger players often think that the only positions that really need to know how to dribble well are the guards since they take the ball up the court most often. That view is totally mistaken! Everyone on a basketball team should be a polished dribbler. To skimp on this skill as an individual is to diminish your team's ability to control the ball.

Basic Body Position

Fundamental to good dribbling technique is the correct body position as you bounce the ball on the floor. You should crouch with your knees slightly bent, your shoulders forward, but your back relatively straight. Hold your head up, try to be as relaxed as possible, and keep your eyes alert to the activity of teammates and defensive men alike. As you dribble the ball with one hand, the opposite hand and arm should be out away from the body for balance and to protect the ball from being stolen by the defense. Think of the free arm as a kind of bumper/outrigger

The Proper Dribbling Stance

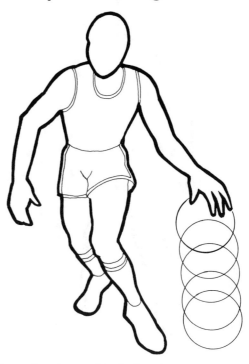

Hold your head up and look ahead

and try to keep it flexible—not stiff or rigid—as you dribble.

The crouch position allows you to control the ball better than the upright position because the ball stays low to the floor and is less likely to bounce away from you or be stolen. It also allows you to move with the ball more quickly.

How to Dribble

When dribbling, you should always use your fingertips—the palm of the hand should never touch the ball. Holding the ball in one hand, place your other hand on top of the ball with the fingers spread apart. Now bring the ball to your dribbling side, take the holding hand away and start to dribble. Keep your arm and wrist relaxed, and, as you continue to bounce the ball, use a pushing rather than a slapping motion. You'll soon find that the best way to bounce the ball is to flex your wrist, letting the forearm provide the motion, and to control the direction of the

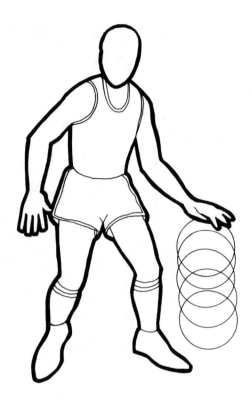

(A) The left-handed dribble

(B) The right-handed dribble

bounce with your outstretched fingertips. If you're dribbling well, only those last digits—the fingertips—will be touching the ball; the rest of the fingers never come in contact with it.

From the very moment you begin to learn to dribble, keep your head up, stay low, and *don't look at the ball!* In a game situation, you want to be able to see the defense and, of course, your teammates. You can't do that with your eyes locked on the bouncing ball. Look forward, not down. If you practice dribbling that way, you'll more quickly develop confidence in your ballhandling ability.

Changing Hands While Dribbling—The Crossover Dribble

Once you feel comfortable dribbling with either hand, it's time to learn how to change hands as you dribble. Being able to change hands is essential during nu-

merous offensive maneuvers and can also help you get out of trouble when you find yourself under tight defensive pressure.

Let's say you're dribbling the ball with your right hand. To switch the ball to your left, make your right hand's last, or transition dribble, much lower and shorter than usual, and angle it, using your fingertips, toward your left hand. The left hand crosses forward to receive the ball after the low bounce and to continue to dribble off the fingertips. Never try to change hands while dribbling the ball high and in front of you. The defense will surely steal it from you.

Walking and Running While Dribbling the Ball

Let's assume that you can dribble the ball with either hand and switch the ball from hand to hand while dribbling. You are now ready to learn how to dribble the length of the court while walking. The most important elements in this phase of your dribbling progress are 1) staying low in order to maintain control of the ball, 2) keeping your head up so you can see where you're going, 3) dribbling the ball on your fingertips. As you start to get the hang of dribbling the full length of the court and back, try the "dribbling-the-lines" drill described on page 49. It will help you practice changing hands on the dribble while walking.

After mastering the dribble while walking, try to dribble while running about half speed. The same elements of staying low, keeping your head up and dribbling the ball on your fingertips apply here more than ever, and you must also be sure to keep your weight forward by running on your toes and the balls of your feet.

You'll find that controlling the ball becomes more difficult as you dribble on the run because the natural tendency is to straighten up instead of staying low. The "seven-chairs" drill, described on page 58, is a beautiful means of learning how to dribble and change hands on the run.

I can't stress enough the importance of everyone on a team, big players and small, learning how to dribble well. Once you've mastered the elements of walking, running, staying low, keeping your head up, and changing hands while dribbling, you're ready to learn some specific types of dribbles which can boost your offensive capabilities immeasurably.

Types of Dribbles

There are five different types of dribbles which can be of tremendous advantage to you depending on the situation. They are:

- *the change-of-pace dribble*
- *the change-of-direction dribble*
- *the behind-the-back-dribble*
- *the crossover dribble* (already discussed on page 38)
- *the reverse dribble*

Let's look at each:

1. **The Change-of-Pace Dribble.** The change-of-pace dribble is one of the greatest aids to successfully executing offensive maneuvers. Players from high school to the pros use it, and it's one of the marks of a polished dribbler. It involves changing *both the height of the ball's bounce and the speed and direction of foot movement.* As often as not, a player will use the change-of-pace to get free of a defensive man, usually by speeding up the ball's bounce (in effect, lowering the height of each bounce) and changing his foot movement from a walk or a trot to a sudden sprint.

You can learn the change-of-pace dribble, too, and it's best to start by learning to control the height of the ball's bounce. In the dribbler's crouch, start by dribbling the ball at normal height (about thigh level), then suddenly lower your hand and dribble the ball only as high as your knee. Notice how the dribble speeds up? You've just changed its pace. After getting the feel for how to make the ball bounce faster or slower, start combining the dribble with different walking or running movements. Walk first, dribbling the ball at normal height, then surge to a run, simultaneously speeding up the dribble (lowering the height of the ball's bounce). Trot, dribbling the ball at an appropriate pace; then sprint, and notice how *you have to change the pace of your dribble in order to avoid losing control of the ball.* Another way of saying this is, the height of the dribble changes depending upon how fast you are moving your feet. Once you can coordinate dribbling height with foot speed, once you can change each at will, you are on your way to becoming an inspired change-of-pace dribbler. Practice your foot-speed/dribbling-height combinations; learn to change the pace of your movement in any direction. The more combinations of movement and pace-change you can throw at a defender, the tougher you will be to defend.

2. **The Change-of-Direction Dribble.** How many times have you seen a topnotch dribbler lull his man into thinking that he's going to continue dribbling in one direction, only to fool him by suddenly changing hands on the next dribble and darting off in a different direction? That's the change-of-direction dribble, and it's most effective when used in combination with the change-of-pace. The keys to the change-

of-direction dribble are 1) good acting, and 2) good footwork. First, you have to make your man think you'll continue in a straight line, and then, once he's been lulled, you have to plant your pivot foot (it doesn't matter which) and push off of it as quickly as possible as you change dribbling hands. The better the actor you are, the better your chances of throwing your opponent off stride.

3. **The Behind-the-Back Dribble.** Tricky, flamboyant, and fun to watch, the behind-the-back dribble is a risky maneuver that should not be used unless it's your only means of getting away from a defender.

Basically, the move entails shifting the ball behind you from one dribbling hand to the other, and you make the shift by 1) dribbling the ball to the dribbling hand's side, 2) pushing the ball behind you at an angle so that it bounces toward the receiving hand, 3) shifting your weight away from the receiving hand so that the hand can receive and control the ball more easily.

Good behind-the-back dribblers make the maneuver look fluid and effortless, but it's a difficult move to master and should not be used in a game unless you're confident you can perform it on every try.

4. **The Reverse Dribble.** How many times have you seen an offensive player make a move along the baseline and then get cut off by the defense? If that offensive player does not know how to pivot away from the defensive man and continue his dribble, he does not know how to execute a reverse dribble.

To execute a reverse dribble plant both feet squarely. By doing this you are now free to establish your pivot foot. When you start to make the pivot away from the defense stay low on the dribble and change hands with the ball while moving away from the defensive man. This is a continuous motion and through practice you will be able to make the move fluidly. The keys to the reverse dribble are 1) keep the dribble low, 2) learn to establish the pivot foot (footwork), 3) change hands with the ball.

To practice the reverse dribble the twelve chairs drill (see page 56) can be very helpful to you. The chair that is located on the baseline at the free-throw lane is where this dribble is executed. At first practice the move at half-speed until you get the feel of it. Then practice this dribble every chance you get until it becomes instinctive.

FAKES

You can't expect your opponent to let you do whatever you want on the court, so, once you feel comfortable shooting, passing, and dribbling, it's time to start combining those skills with a variety of fakes. In most game situations, a good fake is the only way you can get into position for the shot you want to take, or to make the appropriate pass or dribble. Good faking is good acting. By faking well, you make your opponent react to something that never actually occurs.

There are numerous different kinds of fakes. They range from simple head fakes to shoulder, eye, ball, and foot fakes and infinite combinations of each of them. Some of the basic fakes are illustrated here for your study. I recommend practicing fakes off of shots, dribbles, and passes.

In developing your fakes, try not to telegraph your movements in advance, lest you lose any advantage the fake might gain for you. Instead, make the fake (or fakes) only at the last possible moment. Also, *never fake out your teammates!* That sounds obvious enough, but what it means is that you should never try a fake in a game that you have not already tried in practice. After all, by faking, you're trying to create an advantage for your team, not a surprise that could lead to a costly turnover. For that matter, there are times when a fake is a wasted motion. Learning to separate those times when it is needed from those when it is not is a matter of practice and experience. But, in general, you should develop your fakes off the shot, pass, and dribble so that they become habit and you can fake at will.

The essence of good faking can be summarized in five rules:

1. *Never telegraph a fake.*
2. *Do not fake too often.*
3. *Protect the ball at all times while faking.*
4. *Study your opponent's moves and fake accordingly.* (For example, if your opponent has a tendency to lean in a certain direction on defense, make a fake in that direction to throw him further off balance.)
5. *Be versatile and creative when faking.* Remember: The best fakers are consummate actors; they never do the expected. They just look as though they do.

Grabbing the defensive rebound

REBOUNDING:
Eight Critical Qualities

Not all shots go into the basket, and that's where rebounding comes into play. In many games, good offensive rebounding is the deciding difference between two teams, and the team that can control both the offensive and defensive boards, as often as not, controls the game. Over the years, I've analyzed what separates the great rebounders from the me-diocre ones, and I've come up with eight critical qualities that every great one has. Interestingly enough, I've discovered that you don't necessarily have to be a 6'11" giant to be a good rebounder. Sure, size helps; but position, desire, and a body balance can serve the shorter player just as well.

Let's look at those eight qualities now with an eye to incorporating them into your total game.

1. *Be a pursuer.* Do not stand still. When the ball is shot, go after the rebound with determination. If

you stand still, in all likelihood you will not get the rebound. Don't be left flat-footed!

All great rebounders think that, once the ball is shot, the rebound belongs to them. This is the kind of attitude that you should develop—it's essential to effective rebounding.

2. *Get a good position.* Positioning yourself properly for a rebound requires anticipating where the ball will come off the rim or backboard once it is shot. To get good position, you must, in an instant, analyze the location on the floor where the shot is taken, the arc of the ball, and the position of the other players; then you must move for the rebound. Needless to say, doing all that takes tremendous intelligence and athleticism.

Try, when you position yourself for a rebound, not to get too far under the hoop, lest you miss the ball entirely. Most of all, though, get to the right spot first!

3. *Maintain proper body balance.* Once you're in position to rebound, your feet should be spread in a stride position about a shoulder's width apart, and your knees should be slightly bent to lower your center of gravity. This position serves two functions: First, it enables you to move sideways as well as vertically, and second, it minimizes the chance of your losing your balance or being moved. Once in this position, stay on your toes and the balls of your feet, and don't get caught flat-footed. You more than likely will be jumping for the ball, and you can't jump effectively from your heels.

4. *Block out your opponent.* Along with good position and body balance, successfully blocking out your opponent is the key element to rebounding. If you're a smaller player blocking out a bigger one, try to get between him and the basket as soon as possible after the shot and keep your hands low so you can feel where he is. If you're a big player blocking out a bigger one, keep your arms and elbows chest high so that they serve as bumpers to hold the bigger player off.

5. *Have desire and be tough.* The great rebounder is one who possesses a bushel-load of desire, and along with that, he cultivates a mental and physical toughness. Rebounding is no skill for the weak or fainthearted. There will be times when you have to go up for a rebound that isn't in your area. By saying to yourself that every ball that doesn't go into the hoop is yours, you'll develop the desire and aggressiveness needed to be a strong rebounder.

6. *Learn to time your jump for the rebound.* All of your positioning, balance and blocking out are wasted if you don't time your jump to coincide with the descent of the ball. Learn to read caroms; know where the missed shot will fall and when. You should also practice jumping many times in rapid succession for those frequent times when the ball does the unexpected and bounces around the rim more than once before it falls.

7. *Once you've grabbed a rebound, protect the ball.* The normal procedure after a rebound is to hug the ball close to your body, about chest high. Sometimes, however, circumstances dictate holding the ball over your head. In heavy traffic, for instance, the taller player risks losing the ball to a smaller one if he holds it chest-high; indeed, by so doing, the taller player eliminates his height advantage. He's far wiser to hold the ball over his head. Too, holding the ball up high is good practice once the opposition has cleared away from you and you want to make an outlet pass to the side to start a fast break.

8. *Develop good hands and fingertip control.* Whenever you go for a rebound, keep your hands and fingers relaxed yet firm. Most often the term "fingertip control" is applied to offensive rebounding, but it has its place in defensive rebounding, too. By having good hands and fingertip control offensively, you can tip the ball to a teammate for a second or third shot; defensively, you can tip the ball to a teammate, or over an opponent's head to yourself, to start a fast break. The point is, the same "soft hands" you've developed as a passer and shooter can serve you equally well as an effective rebounder. Always try to measure yourself against your opponent so that you can keep the rebounding advantage, and remember that the rebounder is an opportunist who, through analysis, calculation, and will, puts himself in precisely the right spot at the right time.

4

Warm-Up Drills

In basketball as in any other sport, the way good players get better, and better players get great is by practicing. But just going out on the court every day and randomly shooting, dribbling, and passing is not enough. Through the years, basketball experts have found that the best way to program a player's muscles into making the proper movement patterns for the game is through the repetition of certain clearly-defined drills.

Having played high school and college basketball well enough to make the pros, I can say from my own experience that the experts are right. Drills are where it's at. They help focus your practice time, even when you're practicing alone, and the discipline you gain from trying to perform them well pays off in numerous benefits, both tangible and intangible, when you find yourself actually playing in a game.

What follows is my list of the Sixteen All-Time Great Warm-Up Drills. Each is designed for a specific purpose, but their overall function is to improve your fingertip control of the ball, your confidence in dribbling and passing, and your personal mastery of every fundamental of the game. Many of the drills can be performed alone or with a training partner, and none takes more than one or two minutes. But simple as they are, these drills can help any player, from high school to the pros, improve his game, and they're worth doing even after your playing career is over. I still do these drills even though I'm retired as a player because they're a great workout, and I enjoy keeping my playing skills sharp.

Remember: Drills are your friends; in the long run they're going to help you, so give them all the love and intensity you've got. Now, let's go.

DRILL 1
A Simple Ballhandling Drill

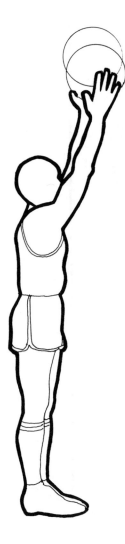

Take the basketball and hold it on the fingertips of your right hand. By using your fingertips as a guide, move the ball from your right hand to your left hand at waist level. Now extend your arms and move the ball from one hand to the other at eye level. Then, without looking at the ball, move it above your head until you feel comfortable with that back-and-forth movement. Finally, move the ball down to about knee level and repeat the back-and-forth motion there. The entire drill—moving the ball from waist to the eyes to above the head to the knees—should be done in a continuous motion for one minute. This is a great exercise for getting the feel of the ball.

DRILL 2
The Dribble-Against-the-Wall Drill

Take the basketball and stand about three feet from a solid flat wall, making sure not to lean forward as you do the following drill: Hold the ball above your head and dribble it off the wall twenty-five times with your right hand, then twenty-five times with your left. Complete the drill by dribbling the ball twenty-five times with both hands together.

The purposes of this drill are several. Not only does it help you get the feel of the ball and improve your fingertip control, it also strengthens your wrists and improves your tipping ability both in offensive and jump-ball situations. You should do the dribble-against-the-wall drill for a maximum of two minutes.

DRILL 3
The Around-the-World Drill

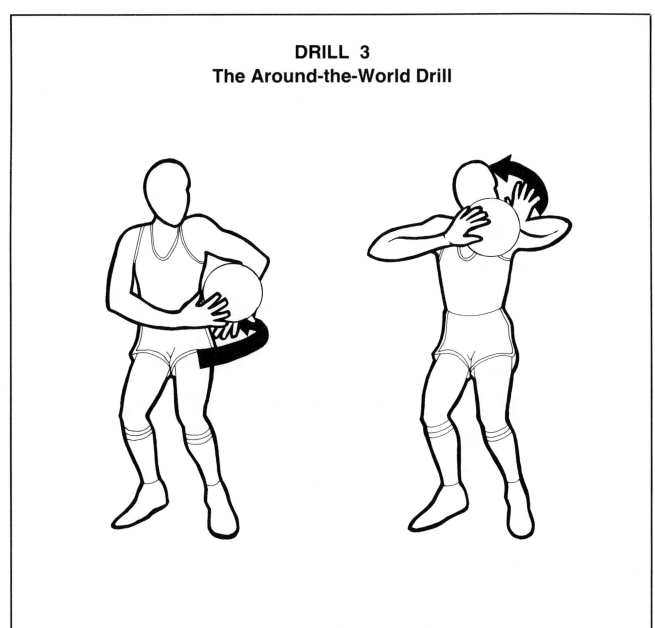

I call this the "around-the-world" drill because of the ball's orbital movement around the body. Simply take the ball and move it around your waist, your knees, and then your neck, all the while holding it with only the fingertips. Listen for a slapping sound as you transfer the ball from one hand to the other. If you hear one, it's a sign that you're using your palms to handle the ball, which, as you remember, is incorrect technique. The slapping sound will disappear only when you start using your fingertips.

The purpose of this drill is to help you get the feel of the ball and to aid you in the development of an effective behind-the-back pass. Move the ball clockwise for one minute, then reverse the movement for a second minute and stop.

DRILL 4
The Between-the-Legs Drill
(Ballhandling Without a Dribble)

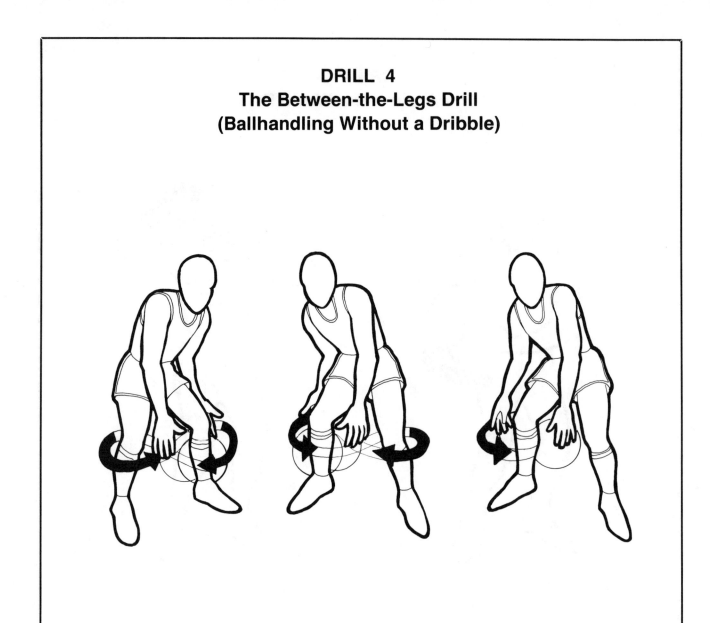

Spread your legs a shoulder's width apart and bend your knees slightly. Now take the ball and move it around one leg and then the other, transferring it from hand to hand to do so. Once you can move the ball at speed around either leg, move it around your legs in a figure eight pattern as shown in the diagram. Try to keep your movements fluid and continuous, and never let the ball touch your palms or the floor.

This is a wonderful drill for developing your ballhandling agility and will serve you well when you practice another between-the-legs dribbling drill, which I'll show you in a few pages. Once again, move the ball in one direction for a minute, then reverse direction for another minute and stop.

DRILL 5
Dribbling the Lines

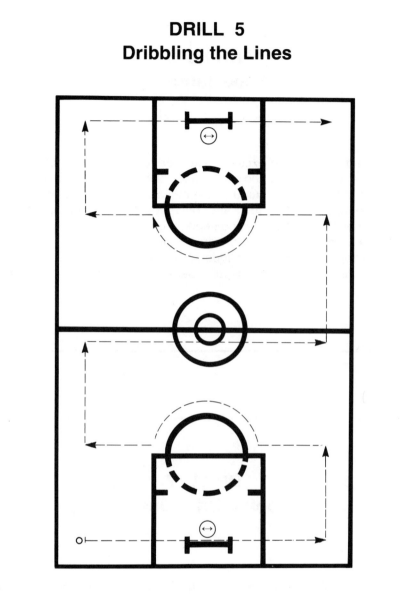

Start in the left-hand corner at either end of the floor and dribble along the lines, following the pattern shown in the diagram and switching hands on the dribble at each left or right turn. Keep your head up as you dribble but stay low so you can control the ball. Try to make your cuts at the corners and around the tops of the keys sharp and precise while maintaining as much speed as you can without sacrificing ball control.

The purpose of this drill is to improve your dribbling technique, and you'll find that it also develops your footwork, particularly on cuts and turns, and increases your ballhandling confidence tremendously. Big men will find it helpful for curbing any tendency they may have to dribble the ball too high, and all players can benefit from having to dribble the ball with their "weak" hand.

DRILL 6
Rope Jumping

Any athlete should jump rope. It's an excellent exercise for improving your agility, footwork, and jumping ability, as well as your stamina and cardiovascular fitness. What's important in rope jumping is developing a routine that will last for three to five minutes without a break.

Start by jumping the rope with both feet, and, once you feel warmed up, alternate your jumps from one foot to the other. When you get good enough, crisscross the rope in front of you and also try jumping with a backward, rather than a forward swing.

Some athletes jump rope while wearing padded ankle weights, but I discourage this practice as the weights can cause muscle and ligament pulls, particularly around the area of the knee.

DRILL 7
The Tipping Drill (One Player)

Set yourself in the rebounding position and toss the ball high against the backboard. Tip the ball against the backboard for ten repetitions, and on the last tip, bank the ball into the basket. Repeat the procedure using your left hand and then both hands for a total of thirty tips. When tipping with both hands, angle the ball off the backboard so that you have to shift from one side of the hoop to the other. On every rebound, you should try to tip the ball at the very peak of your jump.

Besides developing your ability to make a second or third effort when rebounding, this important little drill will improve your jumping ability, your timing on rebounds, and your ball control on the tip.

DRILL 8
The Backboard Drill (Two Players)

With a training partner standing on one side of the basket and you on the other, toss the ball high against the backboard so that the rebound drops in the direction of your partner and he can tip the ball off the board and back to you. The two of you then tip the ball back and forth at least ten times using first your left hand, then your right hand, then both hands.

You should concentrate on keeping your hands up and tipping the ball at the peak of your jump with your fingertips. When landing, be sure to bend your knees and land on your toes and the balls of your feet so that you're instantly ready to go up again. This bent-knee, on-the-toes and the balls of your feet landing is critical in order to make a second or third rebounding effort in game situations.

Practiced regularly, this drill will improve your jumping and tipping ability, your agility, your timing on rebounds, and overall physical condition.

DRILL 9
The Rebounding Power Drill (One Player)

The rebounding power drill starts exactly the same way as the tipping drill. Set yourself in the rebounding position and toss the ball high against the backboard. Jump for the ball and at the peak of your jump, grab the ball in two hands with a downward motion and land on the floor, taking up as much area as possible. Then gather yourself so that you cannot be knocked off balance and "power" yourself back to the basket and put the ball in. In rebounding, this is called the "power move," and to do it you must make sure to protect the ball by keeping it at chest level when you land with it and not lowering it toward the floor where it can be stolen or knocked away. In the same way that you did during the tip drill, always land on your toes and the balls of your feet, not the soles of your feet. When practicing defensive rebounding, try to turn in midair after grabbing the rebound so that you're in position when you land to make the outlet pass.

DRILL 10
Jumping the Stick

Of all the drills described here, I have found this one to be the most helpful in improving a player's agility. I have known many players who dislike this drill, but the reason for their aversion is that they've never learned how to do it properly. Once you know how to jump the stick well, I guarantee it will become one of your favorite drills.

To perform the jump-the-stick drill, set out two chairs and place a broom handle or yardstick between them at seat level. (You can also use a high jumping bar and standards and adjust the bar to any height desired.) Stand sideways to the bar and begin leaping back and forth over it, at first in repetitions of ten at a time. You'll quickly discover that the only way you can jump with any speed or rhythm is to land on your toes and the balls of your feet. After the first day of jumps, add ten more every other day until you are doing forty to fifty jumps at a clip.

This is a beautiful drill for developing your agility, jumping ability, body control, and overall condition. Big slow mature players benefit enormously from this drill, and it can also improve the coordination of boys and girls who are big for their age.

DRILL 11
The Between-the-Legs Dribbling Drill

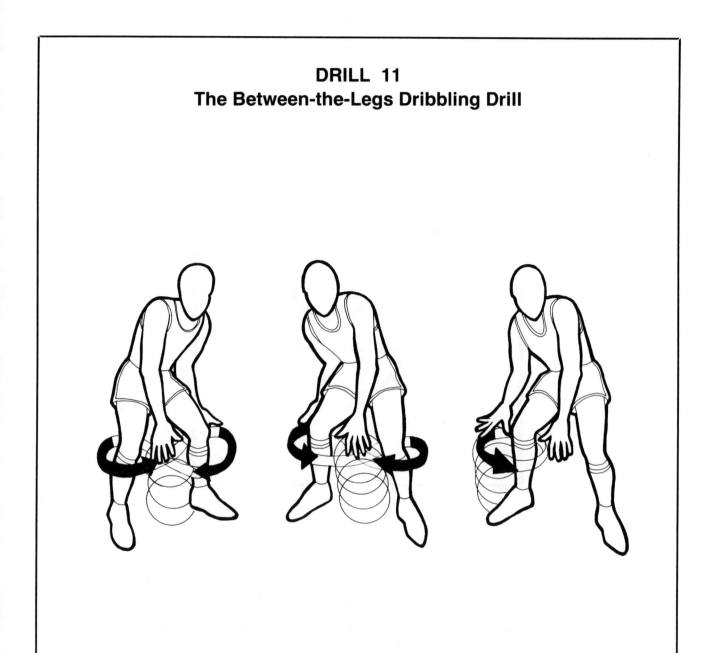

Assume the correct stance for dribbling: knees bent, back lowered, head up. Using your fingertips, dribble the ball back and forth in front of you, transferring it from your right to your left hand. Now dribble the ball behind and around one leg, then behind and around the other, working the ball from one hand to the other to do so. Once you can dribble around each leg separately, complete the drill by dribbling around the legs in a figure eight pattern as shown. You should eventually try quickening the dribbling tempo so that you are dribbling around your legs as fast as you can.

  This is an excellent drill for improving your dribbling skill, footwork, and hand-eye coordination. A minute for each phase is dribbling time enough.

DRILL 12
A Passing Drill (Six Players)

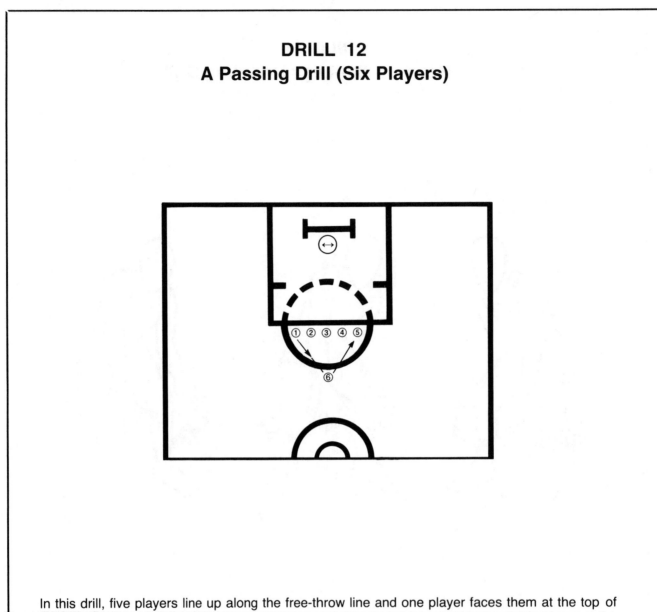

In this drill, five players line up along the free-throw line and one player faces them at the top of the key. A player with one of two balls makes a two-handed chest pass to the single player at the head of the circle. A split second before receiving the ball the player at the head of the circle has passed his ball to the player at the end of the line. When one of the balls is passed from the middle man along the free-throw line to the player at the top of the key, then the receiver begins the sequence over again by passing the ball back to a player at either end of the line. Each player has a turn as the single man, and everyone includes a forward step with his chest pass as was taught on page 31.

This drill quickly improves hand-eye coordination and peripheral vision when passing and is a great way of instilling a sense of teamwork and camaraderie among players.

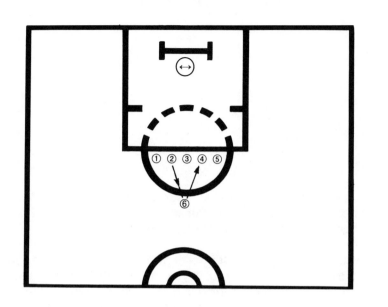

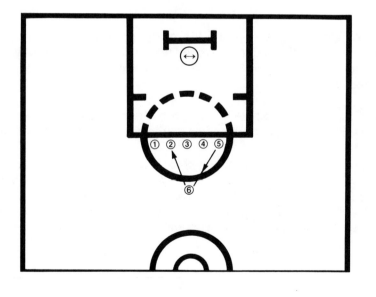

DRILL 13
The Twelve Chairs Drill

Place twelve chairs on the basketball court as follows: three on the sideline, one near the free-throw lane on the baseline, one at the top of the key, and one at the free-throw line, and the other six in the same arrangement at the other end of the court (see diagram).

Step 1: Starting on a sideline with three chairs in front of you, dribble toward them, using a change-of-pace dribble at the midcourt line until you reach the first chair. Fake to the inside, plant your inside foot, push off in the opposite direction, and dribble around the outside of the chair. Continue on in a slalomlike fashion to the second and third chairs. Now, heading toward the fourth chair, which is near the baseline, make a reverse dribble and shoot any of the following shots: a jump shot, a fall-away bank shot, a jump shot dribbling into the paint (the three-second area), a regular lay-up or a reverse lay-up. After shooting retrieve the ball and dribble up the middle of the court.

Step 2: When you reach the chair at the top of the opposite key, fake, plant the pivot foot, change direction by pushing off and dribble around the chair. You immediately encounter the chair on the free-throw line. Use a crossover dribble to continue to the basket and make a running right- or left-handed hook shot.

Step 3: After making the shot, dribble the length of the court as fast as you can and make the same maneuvers as in step 2, only this time use your opposite hand on the hook shot.

Step 4: After making the shot, drive the length of the court, dribble up the far side of the floor, and repeat the maneuvers you performed in step 1. You can do the Twelve Chairs Drill by yourself or with a teammate (or teammates) alternating who takes the shot.

This is a superb all-around conditioning drill, and when done properly can quickly improve advanced dribbling skills, hand-eye coordination, peripheral vision, and teamwork.

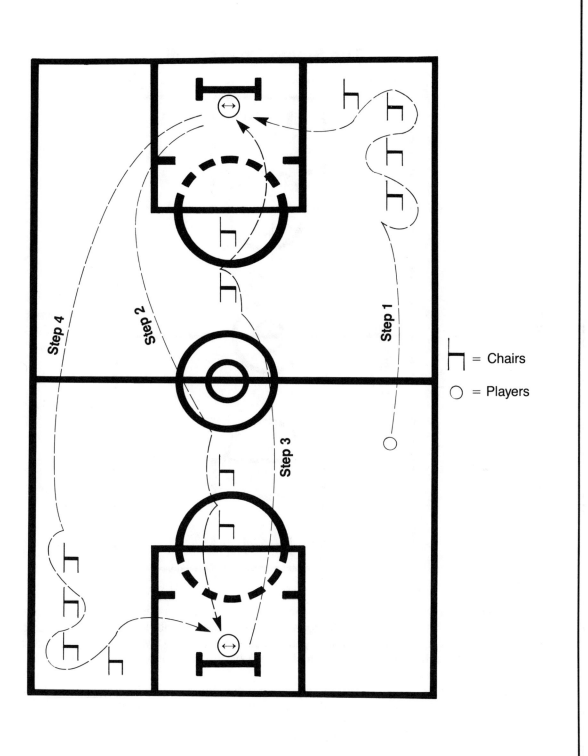

Step 4

Step 2

Step 1

Step 3

⊢ = Chairs

○ = Players

DRILL 14
The Seven Chairs Drill

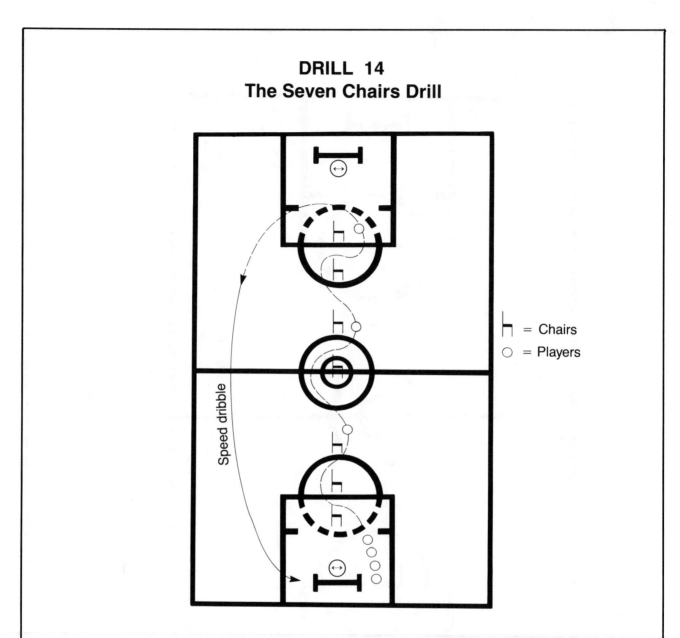

Place seven chairs three or four feet apart in a straight line up the middle of the court. Start at the baseline, and, at first at a comfortable speed, but later, faster, dribble the ball in a zigzag pattern around each chair. To control the dribble, you must keep your body low and change hands between the chairs. After reaching the last chair, dribble back up the court at a sprint (this is called a "speed dribble") and shoot a lay-up.

This is one of those drills you can do on your own that can help you improve your dribbling skills in no time. Personally, I like the way the drill forces you to stay low and makes you concentrate on your hand and footwork. Don't neglect the lay-up at the end of the drill. It's designed to help you improve your scoring percentage on the fast break.

DRILL 15
The Combination Ballhandling Drill

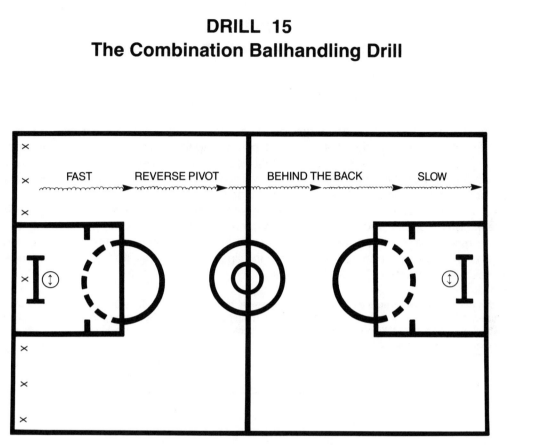

FAST   REVERSE PIVOT   BEHIND THE BACK   SLOW

X = Players

Seven players, each with a basketball, line up across the baseline. A coach or fellow player then tells the players what combination of dribbles he desires. A typical combination might include: 1) slow dribbles, 2) behind-the-backs, 3) between-the-legs, 4) reverse dribbles, 5) fast dribbles. If the coach or other player has a whistle, he can blow it when he wants a change in the dribble, or he can designate the free-throw line, the top of the key, the midcourt line, etc. as markers for changing to the next dribble.

All players should move forward together, reverse and repeat the combination on their return from the opposite end of the court. Eventually, a coach can require that players make up their own routines, but the group should move together nonetheless.

The combination drill is one of the best means I know for improving footwork, ballhandling, and dribbling skill, and it's a good conditioning exercise, too, when the coach speeds the pace. When introduced properly—not too fast at first, not too many combinations—it's a beautiful confidence-builder, especially for the younger, undeveloped player.

DRILL 16
The Figure-8 Drill (Team Drill)

The team is lined up into three equal groups at one end of the court. Moving up the floor with the ball, the first player in the middle starts the drill by passing the ball to either wing. After making that pass, the player goes behind the player he just passed to. The weaving pattern continues all the way down the floor until the players reach the opposite basket. Without stopping, the players then turn around and continue the weave all the way back.

This is a popular team drill and can be done with a medicine ball or heavyweight ball as well as a basketball. For maximum benefit, it's essential that each player go immediately behind the player he has passed to. In general the Figure-8 drill is designed to improve ballhandling skills, passing, and timing, but if the drill is run with the lines widely separated, it also becomes a great tool for learning and controlling the fast break.*

*Again, this drill can be run using a medicine ball, heavyweight ball, or basketball. In addition, my high school coach, Don Morris, used to have his players wear cotton work gloves (obtainable at hardware stores) while running the Figure-8. His theory was that if you could perform the drill with gloves on, think how much better your technique would become with them off. This gloves-on drill was a great confidence-booster!

5

On Coaches and Coaching

In recent years, coaching basketball has become something of a science. With the advent of videotape supplemented by detailed scouting reports, coaches today are better able to diagnose their opposition's strengths and weaknesses and draw up their game plans accordingly. In the 1980 NBA Championship Series, for example, the Los Angeles Lakers studied videotapes of the Philadelphia 76ers and adjusted their offense to capitalize on certain of the Sixers' defensive weaknesses. The result was an easy championship for the Lakers—and a boost in the sale of videotape equipment to every other team in the league!

The technology has its value, but ultimately basketball teams are directed by people—coaches—and there are more things that a coach can teach a player than any piece of videotape equipment can. Many coaches seem to be forgetting this fact. Every coach knows, for example, the importance of recognizing his strengths and weaknesses. And yet, today there are coaches at every level—from youth leagues to the pros who have come to feel that a player's weaknesses are largely uncorrectable. They concentrate on developing the player's strengths, and as a result end up seeing their negative assessments fulfilled because the player's weaknesses eventually do become uncorrectable.

As you might guess by now, I am *not* a believer in leaving a player's weaknesses alone. Most players' weaknesses are in the fundamentals—shooting, passing, dribbling, faking, and rebounding—and, contrary to some current thinking, can be improved. If you're a coach, I recommend that you make your team practice these fundamentals every day. From my own coaching experience, I've found that the best way to build players' strengths and overcome their weaknesses is by drilling the fundamentals at game speed. Only in that way do the fundamentals become second nature to the player. If you're a high school coach, I recommend that fully half your practice sessions be devoted to the fundamentals. High school-age players are easily the most coachable: still young enough to have their weaknesses turned around before they develop into bad habits.

It's a gross mistake and a disservice to the player who has a few lopsided talents to capitalize on that player's abilities without correcting his weaknesses. More and more, basketball may be becoming a game of specialists—players who can do only one or two things, like dunk or dribble, exceedingly well. But I feel there is still room in this game for the player who can do it all, and I urge you coaches out there to consider what you're doing—to your players and to the game—by going the specialization route.

TYPES OF COACHES

A coach may be no better than the players he's provided, but he's also no better than the respect he commands from those he coaches. There are no formulas for a coach to gain his team's respect. He either gains it or he doesn't. Basketball knowledge helps, but all the basketball knowledge in the world can't bring a team together and make it do what a

Giving a clinic for the developing player

coach wants it to do if the team isn't willing to listen to the knowledge's source.

From studying them over the years, I've concluded that there are basically two kinds of respected coaches in basketball: *the player's coach* and *the disciplinarian coach.* Of course, there are coaches who are a little of each type (more on them later), but, year after year, the successful coaches seem to fit these two general patterns.

I think it's worthwhile for coaches and players to understand the characteristics of these two distinctly different coaching styles. After all, you players out there will probably, in the course of your careers, encounter both types of coaches. Understanding their mentality can help you adapt to their style of play. And if you're a coach, you can profit from consciously knowing which category you fit. No matter whether a coach is player-oriented or a disciplinarian, he's ultimately like a theatrical director, con-

sciously bullying, cajoling, or coaxing the best performance from his charges that he can. In that respect, if you don't know yourself, how can you expect your players to know you, let alone respect you? The successful coach, whether a player's coach or a disciplinarian, is a student of hard-earned self-knowledge. He imparts that thirst for self-discovery in all his players, and the players automatically respect him for who he is.

The Player's Coach

This is the coach players love to play for. He understands the players' moods, can act like one of the guys, and is open to suggestions during time-outs because he knows that the players, with their on-court vantage, have a better feel for what's happening in a game than he does, watching from the bench. Players respect the player's coach because they like him, and they'll play hard for him because he never lets them down. In practice, he stresses the fundamentals and the importance of good mental preparation before a game, and he can be a disciplinarian if players try to take advantage of his likability. Thanks to his understanding of his players, perhaps his biggest asset is his ability to make adjustments to their strengths and weaknesses in game situations. The player's coach is often a cheerleader, quick to praise and encourage, and his optimism for the team's success spills over onto every player.

The Disciplinarian Coach

This is a coach who likes to run the "whole show." He calls the plays from the sidelines and doesn't normally invite input from his players. Sometimes disciplinarian coaches are excessively rigid, but the ones who know what they're doing can provide an invaluable experience for the high school or even grade school player, instilling a sense of discipline and hard work in him that he can carry over through his entire career. Most disciplinarian coaches have systems, but the best ones know when to adjust the system to fit a given game situation. Lack of flexibility is the disciplinarian's worst enemy (in the pro ranks the inflexible coach rarely lasts a season). But if he is a realist and recognizes his bond to the rest of humanity (and many disciplinarian coaches don't!), his greatest coaching asset is his ability to help his players become better people.

The Combination Disciplinarian-Player's Coach

Regardless of the type of coach you are, if you're human, there are times when you'll reverse your philosophy. Basketball seasons are long, and some-

Setting up a play for the last shot

times when the team is in a slump, a reverse approach to coaching is the only thing that will pull the team out of it. Don't worry about reversing yourself: If you're an honest coach and care about your team's problems, your players will respect you for the flexibility you demonstrate. I know from my own experience as a professional player that the coach who tightened the reins when they needed tightening, and loosened them when they needed loosening, was a coach I wanted to give 100 percent for every night. Sure, you should demand quality from your players, but stay flexible. Don't scar a kid for life by haranguing him further when he's already down. Keep your coaching constructive and strive to get the most out of every player's ability.

Of course it helps to know what you want your team to do, in a game, in practice. The following is a true story with an ending that I think can be of benefit to any coach.

Recently I was the featured speaker at a high school sports banquet in Teaneck, New Jersey. After the ceremonies, a middle-aged man with a troubled look on his face approached me and said, "Butch, can I talk to you for a minute?" I didn't have a long drive home that night, and the man seemed anxious to speak. "Sure," I said. "Want to sit down?"

It seems the man was a youth league basketball coach, enthused about the game because his thirteen-year-old son was playing it and loving it, but troubled because, in his words, "I don't know what the heck I'm doing. Sure, I know the positions, and I've got the kids playing a man-to-man defense, but our practice sessions are a joke. I have the kids shoot lay-ups for a while, then shoot around the key; then after that we have an intrasquad scrimmage and call it a day. Frankly, I feel I could be doing more with our practices, but what should I be doing? And how do I go about doing it?"

I told the man he wasn't alone. In my travels around the country I meet lots of youth coaches hungry for ways to make their practice sessions more productive for their players. I pointed out to the man that his enthusiasm is the key ingredient to constructive coaching. If a coach is enthusiastic and patient with his players, the rest is easy—and fun. All he has to do is work up a meaningful practice plan and execute it with his players, and his team is on its way toward developing its true potential.

"It's that easy," I said to the man. "And that difficult."

"Would you help me work up a practice plan?" he asked.

I said I would.

What follows is the upshot of that conversation in Teaneck: a five-day practice flow that incorporates all sixteen of the drills that we just covered. None of the sessions lasts longer than ninety minutes, and each is designed to maximize practice time for every player on the team. I recommend that coaches use the flow as a basic guide and not hesitate to mix and match the drills where they feel that different combinations are appropriate. Remember, though, if you're a coach, that enthusiasm and patience are all. Never overwork a player and make sure everyone gets a chance to play.

A COACH'S FIVE-DAY PRACTICE GUIDE

Day One

1. Stretching routine (see chapter 8): 10 minutes

2. Warm-up drills: 10 minutes
   a. Ball-handling drills #1 and #3
   b. Dribbling drills #4 and #5
   c. Passing drill #12

3. Lay-up drill: 5 minutes
   a. Right-handed
   b. Left-handed
   c. Lay-up down the middle lane using the board

4. Shooting drill: 5 minutes
   Spot shooting from the corner to around the key area

5. Work on offensive plays: 10 minutes
   a. Plays against man-to-man defense (see page 95)
   b. Plays against zone defenses (see pages 98-102)
   These plays are run without a defense.

6. Scrimmage: 20 minutes
   Be sure to stop the scrimmage to explain and correct player's mistakes the moment they happen

7. Free-throw shooting: 5 to 10 minutes
Keep a record—it keeps the players honest!

Day Two
1. Stretching routine: 10 minutes

2. Warm-up drills: 10 minutes
   a. Ball-handling drills #1 and #2
   b. Dribbling drills #4 and #5
   c. Passing drills #12 and #16

3. Lay-up drill: 5 minutes
   a. Right-handed
   b. Left-handed
   c. Lay-up down the middle lane using the board

4. Shooting drill: 5 minutes
   Spot-shooting from the corner and at the free-throw line

5. Work on offensive plays: 10 minutes
   a. Plays against man-to-man defense
   b. Plays against zone defense
   These plays are run without a defense

6. Scrimmage: 20 minutes
   Be sure to stop play to explain and correct players' mistakes the moment they happen

7. Free-throw shooting: 5 to 10 minutes
   Keep a record

Day Three
1. Stretching routine: 10 minutes

2. Warm-up drills: 15 minutes
   a. Ball-handling drills #1, #5, and #14
   b. Jumping drills #7 (1 player), and #8 (2 players)
   c. Condition drills #13 and #16

3. Lay-up drill: 5 minutes
   a. Right-handed
   b. Left-handed
   c. Reverse lay-ups using the right and left hands

4. Shooting drill: 5 minutes
   a. Spot shooting off the dribble around the key area and on the baseline

b. Fake one way and dribble a few times for the jump shot

5. Work on offensive plays: 10 minutes
   a. Plays against man-to-man defense
   b. Plays against zone defense
   Spend five minutes without defense, then five minutes with defense

6. Scrimmage: 20 minutes
   Do not stop the scrimmage; let the team play but spend some time after practice to discuss mistakes

7. Free-throw shooting: 5 to 10 minutes
   Keep a record

Day Four
1. Stretching routine: 10 minutes

2. Warm-up drills: 15 minutes
   a. Ball-handling drills #1, #4, and #5
   b. Passing drills #12 and #16
   c. Conditioning drills #10 and #13

3. Shooting drill: 5 minutes
   a. Spot shooting off the dribble
   b. Fake one way and shoot around the key area; fake one way and shoot going to the baseline

4. Lay-up drill: 5 minutes
   a. Left-handed
   b. Right-handed
   c. Reverse lay-up using the right and left hands

5. Work on offensive plays: 5 to 10 minutes
   a. Plays against man-to-man defense
   b. Plays against zone defense
   Work without defense

6. Work on defense: 10 minutes
   a. Man-to-man defense
   b. Zone defenses

7. Scrimmage: 15 minutes
   Again, let the team play and discuss the mistakes after the scrimmage

Tripling down on the shooter

8. Free-throw shooting: 5 to 10 minutes
   Match the best shooters against each other and have them shoot 25 free throws

9. Work on tipping and rebounding: Drills #8 and #9

Day Five

1. Stretching routine: 10 to 15 minutes
   If there are jump ropes, have the team jump rope the last two minutes

2. Warm-up drills: 15 minutes
   a. Ballhandling drills #1, #2, #4, and #5
   b. Conditioning drills #13 and #14

3. Lay-up drill: 5 minutes
   a. Right-handed
   b. Left-handed
   c. Lay-up down the middle lane using the board

4. Shooting drill: 10 minutes
   a. Spot shooting without the dribble
   b. Spot shooting off the dribble

5. Work on offensive play: 5 minutes
   a. Plays against man-to-man defense
   b. Plays against zone defenses
   Work without defense

6. Work on defense: 10 minutes
   a. Man-to-man defense
   b. Zone defenses

7. Scrimmage: 15 minutes
   Talk about mistakes after practice, but do not hesitate to stop the scrimmage if the mistakes are too blatant

8. Free-throw shooting: 5 to 10 minutes
   a. Divide the team equally and have them hit a designated number of free throws consecutively

9. Work on tipping and rebounding: Drills #8 and #9

SOME ADDITIONAL PRACTICE TIPS TO COACHES

1. For best results, always plan the practice schedule beforehand.
2. Select the drills you are most comfortable with and which you can demonstrate yourself, if possible.
3. Run the drills at game speed, and repeat them so that the players perform them reflexively.
4. Add new drills when the players show signs of mastering the old ones.
5. Discuss the importance of teamwork and the "we" concept.
6. Discuss team rules and regulations so that every player knows what is expected of him.
7. Be enthusiastic and communicate that enthusiasm to your players.

6

TEAM OFFENSE

FOR THE PLAYER
FOR THE COACH

FOR THE PLAYER

In basketball as in other team sports, the team with the most points at the final buzzer wins. In other words, if you haven't noticed, scoring is the name of the game. Over the years, as shooting, passing, and dribbling have become more sophisticated, offensive alignments have changed. The terminology used to describe those alignments is completely different from what it was forty years ago, and team offensive basketball has evolved so that specialized players perform specific designated roles within the context of the total team.

In this chapter I'd like first to define the offensive responsibilities of every position on the court, and then show you how to prepare yourself mentally so that you can get the most out of your position. After that, we'll examine the offensive plays and alignments most used in basketball today, and throughout the chapter we'll learn the importance of playing offense as a team not as a collection of individual players.

THE TEAM: OFFENSIVE POSITIONS

The Point Guard

The point guard runs the offense and is, in fact, an extension of the coach on the floor. He must have an instinctive knowledge of the game, be a good ballhandler and passer, possess speed and quickness of foot, and above all, not have an ego so inflated that it interferes with his basketball judgment, which should be superior to everyone else's on the floor. Normally the point guard receives little publicity for his fine play and his courage in taking a charge defensively, but his coach and teammates know his value to the team.

The Off-Guard

Also known as the number two guard or shooting guard, the off-guard is normally a better shooter than the point guard, able to sink shots in the fifteen to twenty foot range with good consistency. He must know how to move without the ball, be a defensive hound, and he should also be a sufficiently fine ballhandler and student of offense so that he can step in and run the offense if the point guard is being overplayed, or must leave the game.

The Center

The center, along with the point guard, is easily the most important player on the team. Normally the tallest player on the floor, the center must possess quickness, rebounding ability, scoring competence, and defensive leadership. To my mind, the center is both the offensive and defensive catalyst on the floor—always talking to his teammmates and helping out as much as possible, and leading the way when it comes to grabbing rebounds and blocking shots. All of this requires a little meanness, a little arrogance on the center's part. He is king of the paint, or lanes, and must prove, by his manner as much as his action, that that territory is his.

The Small Forward

The small forward is the *most gifted player on the team.* In the professional ranks, he is normally 6'6" to 6'9" tall. He must be quick and fast, an adequate rebounder and good passer, and must be able to play defense anywhere on the floor. Most of all, he must be a good scorer, capable of scoring from anywhere around the key and under the boards. The best forwards can score at will, run the length of the floor on the fast break, and simply take control of the game with their exceptional athletic abilities.

The Power Forward

Like the point guard, the power or strong forward doesn't receive much recognition, because if he's doing his job well, his role as the player who does the "dirty work" for the team is taken for granted. he must be a solid rebounder, both offensively and defensively, an adequate passer, scorer and shot blocker, and a gutsy dribbler and runner, able to go the entire length of the floor on a fast break. Along with the center, the power forward controls the area inside the key, and since he's supposed to stand up to any opposition's drive, offensive and defensive, to the basket, he's often known in basketball parlance as the "enforcer."

The Sixth Man, or "Role" Player

At all levels of basketball, the sixth man has become something of an elite figure. The sixth man is one who has set aside his ego so that he can come off the bench at a moment's notice and do whatever is necessary to help his team win. Sometimes his role calls for him to score, play exceptional defense, or a combination of the two; sometimes he's meant to add rebounding strength. Whatever he's capable of doing, the sixth man is an important component to the game today because he satisfies the coach's quest for an advantage, particularly when the game is a close one. As much as anything else, the sixth man is a spark plug, capable of elevating team tempo when play is slowed or sluggish. A supreme example of this type of sixth man was John Havlicek of the Boston Celtics. His mere presence on the court inspired his team to better play.

Since he doesn't start the game, the sixth man must study the game tempo and prepare himself mentally so that he's able to adjust his play to the flow of the game the moment he steps out on the floor. More than anything else, the sixth man gives his team quality minutes when he plays. His coach, then, must know the sixth man's capabilities and limitations, and must further know how long the sixth man can deliver these quality minutes before losing his effectiveness to the team.

MENTAL PREPARATION

I've given lots of talks and clinics in my time, and one thing I always stress to every player I address is the importance of proper mental preparation for a game. Give or take a few percentage points, basketball is 80 percent mental and 20 percent physical. Sure, God packs more ability into some players' 20 percent than others, but the mental demands of the game are the same for every player.

There are as many ways to prepare mentally for a basketball game as there are basketball players. Some players, for example, go into a deep silence before a game, preferring to focus their minds on the upcoming contest. Others enjoy jabbering to everyone in sight, listening to music: staying loose. Still others choose some kind of balance between silence and sociability. Just so long as it helps you play well, your own mental preparation should be the one that works for you.

After preparing yourself mentally for a game, the concentration needed for actual play is another matter. Because basketball is such a fast paced, emotional game where decisions are made in split seconds, a player can easily lose his concentration anytime. What you must do to play the game effectively is block out everything around you except 1) the action on the court, and 2) your coach's plan for that particular game. Once you have your game face, be all business on the floor and try never to let an official or an opponent upset you. This is part of what I call "playing under control," and besides maintaining your emotional cool, it involves remembering to be a team player. We've all seen teams with one dominant shooter who goes for a bucket every time he handles the ball. He may very well get *his* points in the game, but his teammates don't get theirs, and more often than not the team, scorer included, loses. The fact is, you can maintain a respectable scoring average, help everyone else on the team maintain theirs, and win if you remember to play as part of the team. Stay calm, stay cool, *concentrate:* the points will come naturally during the course of play.

It took me four years as a professional player to realize that if I lost my mental edge, my game suffered. I ceased getting the favorable call from the official, I lost control of myself, my shooting went haywire: I hurt the team. Only by keeping your concentration on the floor and staying cool will you be able to execute when called upon, no matter how tight the situation. In fact, experience has taught me that the mentally prepared team that keeps its concentration during a game and plays unselfishly is one that pulls out the victory that, to everyone else watching, looks like defeat.

LOOKING FOR YOUR SHOT

Every player likes to shoot the basketball—if he doesn't he's playing the wrong game. Every player also has a range on the court within which he feels most comfortable shooting. If you haven't yet noticed your ideal shooting range, start looking for it in practice. Find those spots on the floor from where you can shoot the ball with reasonable accuracy and start taking shots from those spots during games. Your teammates should also know from where you shoot best, and you should know their shooting ranges as well.

Once you've found a shooting range within which you feel comfortable, start concentrating on consistency from that range. What do I mean by consistency? The great jump shooters in the pro ranks practice two to three hundred jump shots a day, and aren't satisfied unless they hit 60 percent or better of the shots. Sixty percent may seem like a high percentage to you, but it's the minimum you should

aspire toward if you want to have, and you want your *teammates* to have, any confidence in your shot.

Learn all the shots so that they're a matter of pure reflex to you, but know your range so that you can shoot effectively from your spots no matter how intense the game. As always, of course, the only way to learn your range and improve upon it is by practice, practice, and more practice.

BASIC OFFENSIVE PLAYS AND PATTERNS

Offensive basketball has never been a simple matter of run and gun—although the play of many teams, even in the NBA, may suggest otherwise. Good offense involves choreography, timing, skill, patience, and above all, simple solid teamwork. Without this ingredient, a team's offense is doomed to mediocrity, no better than that of five amateurs on a pick-up team, each unconcerned with the other's offensive play.

Let's look now at the offensive plays and alignments most used in basketball today. Eventually, as your basketball career progresses, you will play on teams that use all of these maneuvers, and probably others as well. Study them now, practice them with your teammates, and discover for yourself how they translate into a higher percentage of scores—and wins.

GUIDE FOR USING DIAGRAMS

In all the diagrams that follow, I use the standard NBA numbering format wherein each player is designated by a number.

1 = point guard
2 = shooting guard, or off-guard
3 = small forward
4 = strong forward
5 = center

Study this numbering system so that you know which player is which, and read the diagrams carefully so that you understand the sequence of each play. Numbers in parentheses indicate player in possession of the ball.

POSTING LOW: LOW-POST BASKETBALL

As basketball has attracted bigger and taller players, it has become more and more a physical game. Nowhere is this more true today than under the boards. Smart coaches with big strong players now try to create physical mismatches under the boards by posting—that is, positioning—their big players low (close to the basket). Their reasoning is simple: If their big men are bigger and taller than the opponents assigned to guard them, they'll be in perfect position to shoot short bank shots, hooks, and lay-ups over or past their opponents, and if they happen to miss a shot, they're still in excellent position for the offensive rebound.

Not all players are cut out to play low post—again, it's a physical game down there, and even when there's a mismatch, if a coach doesn't feel his man is up to it, he shouldn't post him low. If, however, the man is a quality low-post player, the coach may position him there, even when the man is physically outmatched. Good low-post players can hang in un-der the boards, get their shots off and grab rebounds no matter who is guarding them.

To be a low-post player, you must be very good at playing with your back to the basket, since that is how you position yourself under the boards. You must know where you are on the floor at all times, and you must also know how to shoot the shot, or shots, appropriate to each different area. The most common shots taken when posting low are *the turn-around jump shot, the hook shot, the jump hook shot,* and *the reverse lay-up,* all of which you learned in Chapter 2. You should be able to shoot these shots equally well with either hand, and when working on them in practice, you should try to develop a quick, deft release, because you'll rarely have time under the boards for anything slow.

Once you have your shots down pat, your next concern is taking advantage of your opponent in a game. How do you do this?

It takes hard work because normally the defense is within a ten-foot radius of the basket. Good footwork helps you position yourself for meeting an oncoming pass and taking one of your lethal short shots. Physical strength can help you maintain that

The shaded area indicates the low–post player's best position on the floor.

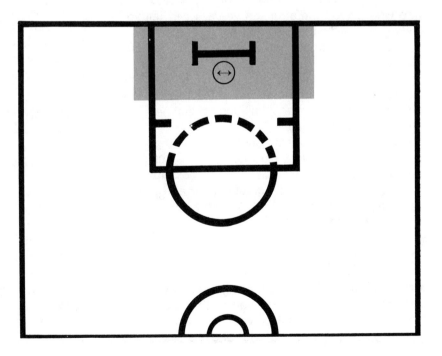

position. There are numerous little tricks that the low-post player knows, both to maintain his position and keep track of his opponent at all times. One involves positioning your feet wide, bending slightly at the waist and keeping the defensive player behind you and "on your hip" so that you can receive the lob pass and go up for a hook or turn-around jumper. This is a difficult series of maneuvers to master—even pro players have trouble with it—but it begins with establishing position and making hip contact with your opponent.

Other tricks the low-poster must know are the fakes necessary for getting off a good jump shot. Of these, the fake jump (often called the double pump) is the most common and most effective. Upon receiving the ball, you quickly move your body up and down as if you are about to shoot a turn-around jumpshot, then, when your opponent is faked into jumping, you actually jump. By then, your opponent is on his way down from his jump and you can get your shot off unmolested, or better yet, draw a foul and a possible three-point play. Of course, when you fake, you don't want your feet to leave the floor, lest you jump twice and be called for an up-and-down, or traveling violation.

The rest of a low-poster's tricks are really a matter of using physical strength to maintain position. As one who played there for ten years, I can tell you without hesitation that play gets hot and heavy under the boards; the upper part of your body, arms and elbows especially, must be strong. In the off-season you should work with weights (see Chapter 8, Off-Season Conditioning), and during the season you should do push-ups and pull-ups to maintain the strength you've gained.

By the way, you guards out there may think that posting low is strictly a big man's game, but think again. More and more coaches are posting their guards low to take advantage of smaller and slower opponents, so you would be wise to sharpen your shooting close to the basket.

CLEARING OUT

Clearing out is a standard means that many teams use in order to take advantage of the opposition, one-on-one. It normally involves the ball going to a player on one side of the floor and the rest of the team moving, or "clearing out," to the other side, up high (away from the basket). By doing so, the team isolates the man with the ball one-on-one against his defender; he is now reasonably free to move in for an easy shot.

Most of the time, the man with the ball is a guard or a forward, particularly skilled at one-on-one offensive play. Centers, though, can also be isolated for an effective one-on-one shot by being posted low.

Of course, clearing out presents the danger that the isolated offensive player could suddenly be double- or even triple-teamed. If that happens, the man with the ball must be alert for the open man (or men) who is now unguarded. He becomes the final option—the safety valve, really—for an open, uncontested shot.

THE BACK-DOOR MOVE

The back-door move is performed by an offensive player when he is being guarded too closely by an individual defender. To go back door, you start by taking a couple steps toward the ball, then stopping; you then make a quick cut to the basket, looking for a pass from your teammate which you can convert into a jump shot or a lay-up. Once you make the back-door move against an overzealous defender, he will stop guarding you so closely—you've burned him once, beaten him to the basket, and if he has any pride, he won't want to be burned again.

THE PICK-AND-ROLL

The pick-and-roll is as old as basketball itself, and yet it has become almost a lost art because players today don't practice it enough. The pick-and-roll can be run by a guard and a forward, a forward and the center, both guards, or both forwards.

Let's say your teammate is dribbling the ball, his man is between him and the basket, and you're setting the pick. First, you should run right up to your teammate's defender and stop, with your knees slightly bent, your feet spread, and your chest just brushing the defender's shoulder. Your teammate can now move away from his defender because you've got that defender effectively blocked—he can

Clearing Out

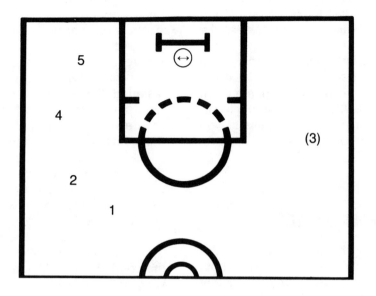

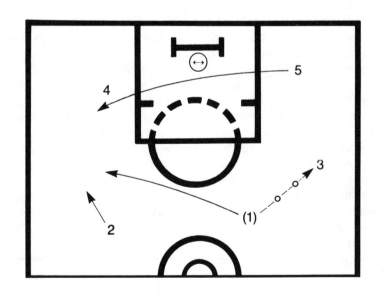

Isolating one player to go one on one against his defender

only run into you. If your defender switches men and starts guarding your teammate, all you have to do is *pivot* and *roll* toward the basket, facing toward the ball, and your teammate can throw either a lob or a bounce pass to you which you can take to the basket for (you hope) an easy score.

The pick-and-roll is a move that every player on your team should know perfectly. Practice it every day and learn to spot the situations in a game when it's most effective—namely, when it will free a teammate for a good shot, or allow him to pass to you on the roll for an even better one.

FOR THE COACH

THE TRANSITION GAME

The transition game has become a major part of basketball offense at every level since it allows both baskets and high percentage shots for the team that uses it. Most of the baskets come off defensive rebounds; the rebounder makes an outlet pass to a teammate who brings it up the floor with his offense. After opposition goals, teams also go into the transition game by putting the ball inbounds quickly and moving it up the court, again before the opposition has time to shift from offense to defense.

The transition game should not be confused with a fast break because it requires the entire team to move quickly, not just one or two players, and it allows for a wider selection of shots, not just the lay-up or typical fast break variants of the lay-up.

If you and your team use the transition game, be prepared to do a lot of running—it's the only way to make the transition game work. Also, be prepared to drop back on defense just as quickly as you move the ball on offense. It's one thing to score an easy basket, but quite another to have an easy basket scored against you. Beyond these requirements, to make the transition game work, everyone on your team must have good judgment and exceptional ballhandling ability. None of you should fear dribbling the entire length of the court.

In today's pro game, the two guards most capable of running their teams' transition games are Magic Johnson and Isiah Thomas. Thomas, at 6'1", possesses amazing quickness and shooting ability—he can score during the transition from virtually anywhere on the floor. These kinds of traits keep defenses off balance. Johnson, at 6'9", is difficult to control on the run, and his height makes it easy for him to see over his defenders and pass or shoot. His height also allows him to haul down the defensive rebound and start the transition from the dribble rather than having to wait for an outlet pass to get it started. Thanks to their exceptional passing ability, both players make their teammates look better in the transition game, and that inspires everyone on the team to run harder and make the transition work.

I like the transition game for many reasons—not the least of which is because it forces players to play instinctively and keeps everyone's head in the game. Besides running and meshing well as a team, the key to a good transition game is moving just as quickly back on defense as offense. When running the transition game offensively, it's critical to keep the court "balanced." Make sure the wing men go wide so that a single defensive player cannot guard two offensive players simultaneously.

THE FAST BREAK

One of the most exciting plays in basketball is the fast break. An effectively executed fast break can be a major weapon in a team's offensive arsenal and can serve as the chief maneuver in their transition game as well. *Speed, quickness, and split-second timing are its key components,* and it should be taught at the earliest levels so that come high school, college, and the pros, it's a move completely familiar to any player.

An intense individual conditioning program emphasizing endurance, speed, and quickness can make you a better fast-break player. Thereafter, you and your teammates must work on good defensive rebounding, adroit ballhandling, and skillful, accurate passing so that your fast break is difficult, if not impossible to defend.

Your team's rebounders must be effective at reading defenses and blocking out so that they can make the proper outlet pass (usually out toward the side-lines, but sometimes directly up the middle) to start the fast break. There must be at least three competent ballhandlers and passers on the team, and

Driving to the basket at the end of a fast break

all five players must have enough court sense to know where every one of their teammates is at any given moment, and enough mental quickness to pass without delay as the team moves from defense to offense.

Contemporary basketball has seen the emergence and development of two specific and highly different ways of running the fast break: *the sideline fast break,* and *the three-lanes fast break.*

The Sideline Fast Break

The sideline fast break is the more structured of the two, usually preplanned and called by the coach during a time-out or a dead-ball situation. Unlike the three-lane break where players run as fast as they can to gain an advantage on the defense, the sideline break is slower and more controlled and tries to gain its advantage by creating defensive mismatches.

It begins usually with the center rebounding the ball and making an outlet pass to the point guard. The guard dribbles down the sideline looking for the shooting guard who started down the same side of the court the moment the outlet pass was thrown. This is the initial movement for running the break.

Once the point guard is over the midcourt line and the shooting guard is down in the corner (still on the same side of the court), the point guard passes to him. The point guard should not stop his dribble and should not pass until he knows the shooting guard is in position and ready. The shooting guard now has the option of shooting a jump shot or looking for the small forward who is posting low nearby. If the shooting guard does not like either of these options, he passes back to the point guard.

After passing the ball back to the point guard, the shooting guard does what is called a shuffle-cut (literally a shuffling, cutting movement) behind the small forward and will look for a pass from the point guard. If he is not thrown the ball, he continues across the baseline to the other side of the court. The point guard now considers a pass to the small forward, who is posting low.

If the point guard cannot pass the ball to the small forward (if the small forward is too heavily guarded), he looks to the other side of the court (known in basketball as the weak side, because the ball isn't

The Sideline Fast Break

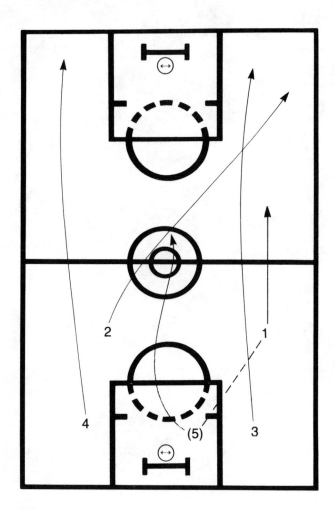

The Initial Team Movement of the Sideline Fast Break

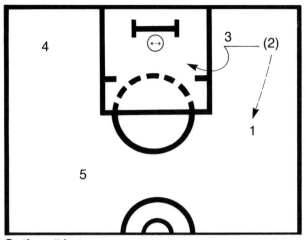

Option #1

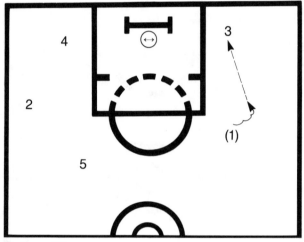

Option #2

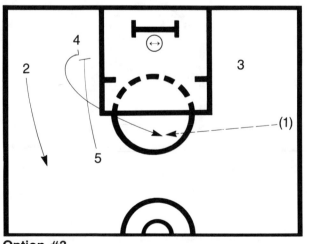

Option #3

there), and passes to the strong forward moving up the key and along the foul line off a pick by the center. The strong forward now has the option of taking the jump shot or looking for the center and the small forward who are now both posting low.

When run properly, the sideline break is beautiful to watch; the floor is always balanced, and the break, as we just saw, presents the offense with a number of high-percentage shooting options. In addition, the sideline break can take advantage of an offense's strengths, especially if they include a center and a forward who play the low post well.

I've always liked the sideline break because the big men on offense only handle the ball when they can attack the defense. The rest of the time they are setting picks and screens that help their smaller teammates get off accurate shots.

Despite its strengths, however, the sideline break does have its potential shortcomings. First, if a team using the break is not adept at handling the ball, it runs the risk of losing it on a steal during one of the break's many passes. Second, some basketball purists argue that bringing the ball up one side of the court kills options that bringing the ball up the middle makes available. Third, the sideline break gives an alert defense the opportunity to double-team the ballhandler or stack, that is, bunch up, in the middle of the lane and thus cancel several of the break's shooting options. Nonetheless, the sideline break has its place, especially when a team wants to set up a high-percentage shot.

The Three-Lanes Fast Break

The three-lanes fast break is the one most commonly seen in the game today, and its main objective is moving the ball up the middle of the court at maximum speed and filling the two outside lanes so that the middle man has the option of either passing or shooting as he approaches the basket. The break usually starts as the result of a turnover, a steal, or a defensive rebound coupled with a quick outlet pass to an open guard. Any player can serve as the middle man in a fast break so long as he is a competent ballhandler (the exception is the center, who normally lacks the foot speed of his teammates). When running the break, the two things players must remember are 1) The players who are running the

The Three-Lanes Fast Break

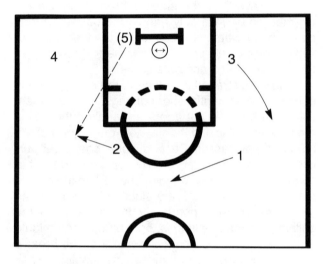

The Initial Team Movement Off the Center's Defensive Rebound

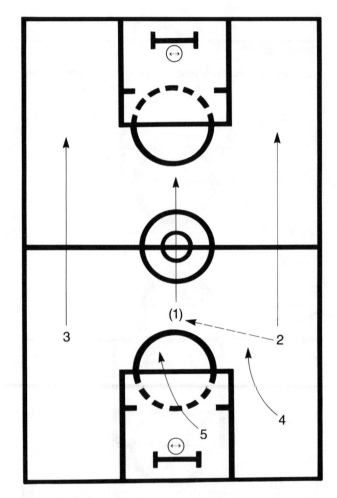

The Ideal Team Movement Upcourt

wings must stay wide to avoid allowing a single defensive man to guard two offensive players in his area, 2) The middle man on the break must stop at the free-throw line unless he is going to penetrate to the basket.

If the three-lanes fast break is run off a defensive rebound, the key to its success is the outlet pass. The pass should be made on the same side of the court as the rebound and as close to midcourt as possible. If the rebounder grabs the rebound in the middle lane, he is free to make his outlet pass to either side of the court.

A good, quick outlet pass moves the ball past the first line of defense. Thereafter, the ball can be advanced in one of two ways: The middle man can dribble it, or he and the two wing men can pass it back and forth as they run up the court. Either method can be effective, and which one a team should use depends entirely on how the defense responds.

What are the fast break's pros and cons? On the plus side, it allows a team to take advantage of its speed, quickness, rebounding ability, and defense, and it also lets a team take a high-percentage shot, usually a simple lay-up. With two men backing up the shooter, a team has the opportunity for a second and sometimes a third shot, and a good break speeds the tempo of the game, which can be useful in demoralizing the opposition, or making up a deficit within a short time. The fast break's problems are that the floor isn't always balanced—the wing men don't always reach their positions fast enough—and it can lead to turnovers if a team lacks ballhandling ability. But with an agile, discerning middle man controlling it, the fast break is a virtually unstoppable bread-and-butter play for the quick of mind and foot.

STRUCTURED OFFENSE: THE UCLA PLAY

So far, we've talked about separate offensive plays: maneuvers that you and your teammates can perform singly or together to respond offensively to different game situations. It's time now to look at some more carefully orchestrated and complex team offenses. These are alignments from which a team can run any number of options, and their value is

multifold. First, a team offense gives every player on a team a clearer idea of what the team will do next offensively. Second, a well-planned offense stands a better chance of cracking a defense than any random individual play. And third, team offenses by their very nature emphasize teamwork, which is the surest way to win games.

When all is said and done, there are essentially two kinds of team offense: structured, and less structured. The structured offense I'd like to show you, called the UCLA play, is designed to work against a man-to-man defense and requires perfect movement among its players to keep the floor balanced at all times. Like other structured offenses, the UCLA tries to create scoring situations rather than simply take advantage of defensive weaknesses, which as we'll see, is the method of the less structured offense.

The UCLA play was made famous in the late '60s and early '70s by coach John Wooden of UCLA. It's designed to take advantage of a team's guards and forwards, but the most important player in this offensive set is the center, who faces the basket and controls the offense's options by means of good passes and fakes. As you'll see when you study the accompanying diagrams, the UCLA presents numerous scoring options, which is why the play has been so successful and why so many college and professional teams have adopted it as their standard offense.

How the UCLA Play Works

After moving the ball past midcourt, the point guard passes the ball to the small forward who is stationed wide of the key. The point guard then cuts to the inside of the center, who is posted high on the same side as the small forward, and looks for a pass and an easy lay-up. If the small forward can't get the ball to the point guard, he waits for him to post low (this is especially effective if the point guard likes to post low and has the height advantage). The small forward then has the option either of passing to the point guard who can take a turn-around jumper or hook shot and perhaps draw a foul, or of passing to the center who can take a jump shot if he is free.

If the small forward passes to the center, the small

forward sets a pick for the point guard who is posted low. The center now has two options: 1) He can pass to the point guard, who comes off the pick looking for a jump shot, or 2) He can pass to the small forward now posted low, who might have a height advantage over his opponent. If the pass goes to the point guard and he does not take the shot off the pick, he looks inside for the small forward posting low.

But those are only two of the options available to the center when he has the ball. There are others. If neither the point guard nor the small forward is open, the center looks to the weak side of the court for the strong forward who is flashing into the foul lane area or paint. This option in particular involves precise timing; the two players can profit from practicing it alone. The center throws either a lob or a bounce pass; in this situation, a lob pass is used if the defender beats the strong forward to his spot in the paint, a bounce pass if the strong forward is free in the middle. If the strong forward is heavily guarded (or if the shooting guard's defender double-teams the strong forward), the center also has the option of passing to the shooting guard stationed to one side of the top of the key.

Once he has the ball, the shooting guard can look inside for the strong forward who has cut toward the basket and is now posting low, or for the small forward who comes toward the foul line after cutting off a pick by the center. If the ball goes to the small forward, he can take a jump shot or look inside for the strong forward and center. And, if all else fails, the players can move to their original positions, the small forward can pass to the point guard, and the entire sequence of options can be tried again.

Normally, that never happens; if everyone on offense moves properly, somebody eventually takes a high-percentage shot. And, even if the shot is missed, the big players are in good position for the offensive rebound.

THE PASSING GAME: A LESS-STRUCTURED OFFENSE

While the UCLA play tries to create offensive advantages by means of preestablished passes and

The Structured Offense: The UCLA Play

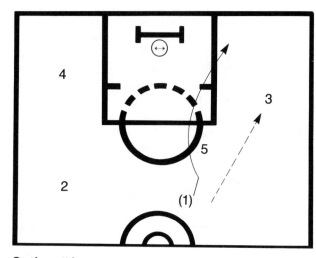

Option #1

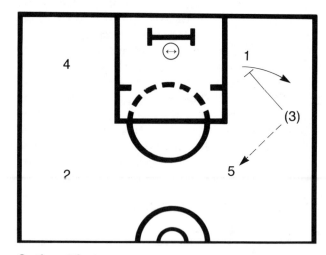

Option #2

player-movement patterns, the passing game offense is less structured and relies on finding offensive advantages based on what the defense does. It's the best offense for creating movement among its players; indeed, this offense disintegrates without movement. And yet, the passing game requires patience to work correctly; players must wait and see what move a teammate will make before they make any moves themselves.

As you'll see when you examine this offense closely, passing and not dribbling is its first priority. The second is maintaining a balanced court via player movement. Executed properly, the passing game offense should keep the middle lane open, thus preventing the defense from "stacking in the paint."

How the Passing Game Works

Once the point guard has brought the ball beyond midcourt, he passes to the small forward, stationed to the right of the key, and then runs to his left to set a pick near the top of the key for the shooting guard. The small forward looks for the shooting guard cutting down the middle lane for a lay-up or stopping at the free-throw area for a jump shot. If, for whatever reason, the shooting guard does not receive the ball, he continues down the lane and comes out on the right side of the court below the small forward, and thus both balances the offensive alignment on the court and keeps the lane open for the offense.

The small forward now looks for the strong forward coming off the pick made by the center from the left or weak side of the court. If the strong forward does not receive the ball immediately for the shot, he continues across the lane and posts low.

Now the small forward passes the ball to the strong forward and sets in motion a special pattern known in basketball as a scissors cut. He starts everything by setting a pick for the point guard, now stationed at the top of the key, who, with the shooting guard, cuts to either side of the strong forward who is posted low. This is the scissors cut. The point guard then sets a pick for the shooting guard and stays on the right side of the court. If the shooting-guard does not receive the ball from the strong forward, he continues to the weak side.

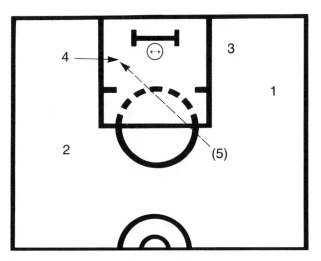

Option #3

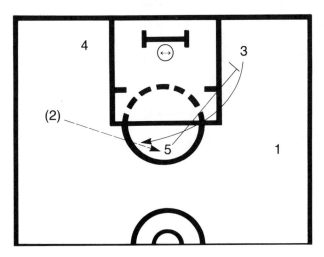

Option #4

The Passing Game:
A Less Structured Offense

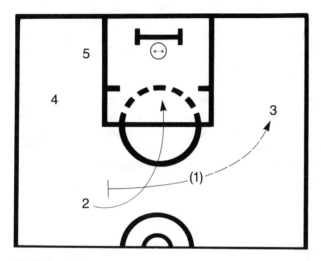

Option #1

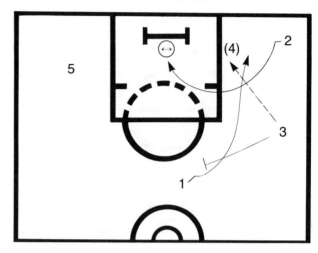

Option #3

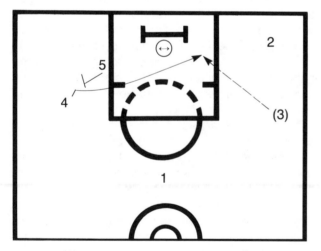

Option #2

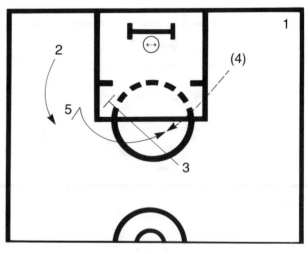

Option #4

If the strong forward has kept the ball after the scissors cut, he can take a shot, *or* he can look to the weak side of the court where the small forward is setting a pick for the center, who is posted high. The center can either receive a pass at the foul line and take a jump shot, or continue down the lane and receive a pass for a lay-up.

In all, as you can see, the passing game works on a series of picks and pass options. If one option doesn't work, a new one takes its place until someone on offense feels he has a percentage shot.

Both of these offenses, the UCLA and the Passing Game, may seem overly complex to you, but each has its internal logic, and each, with practice, works. If your coach decides to install either alignment in your team's offense, no doubt you and your teammates will have to practice the choreography for quite a while until it feels comfortable to all of you. Be patient with yourself and with your teammates during these practice sessions; listen closely to your coach's instruction as he explains the play. In the end, these offenses pay off not only with a higher percentage of points, but with a spirit and a camaraderie within the team that comes from playing well together.

TWO JUMP-BALL SITUATIONS

Jump balls are not the cut-and-dried situations that many teams think they are. When a jumper has the height advantage there are ways to ensure that the ball goes to a teammate, and when a jumper lacks the height advantage, there are ways for his team to effect a steal.

I'd like to show you a standard play for each situation. If your team has the height advantage on the jump, there is absolutely no reason why it shouldn't obtain possession of the ball. If your team lacks the height advantage but plays alert, it still stands a chance of stealing the ball.

The 100 Percent Sure Jump Ball

This is a formation your team should use when it is 100 percent sure it will control the tip. As you can see from looking at the accompanying diagram, the point guard and the strong forward are so positioned

Two Jump-Ball Situations

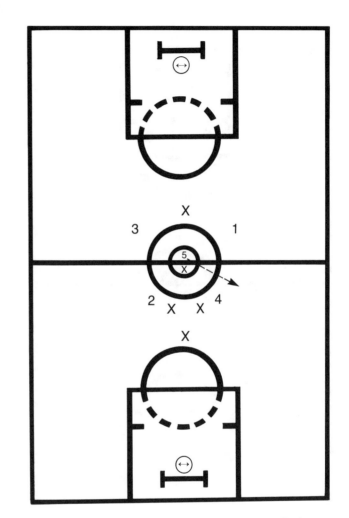

The Sure Tip Play   X = Defense

that they block the nearest defensive players from their side of the court. By tipping the ball to the vacant area between them, the center ensures that either the point guard or the strong forward receives the ball.

The Defensive Gamble on the Jump Ball

This is a defensive formation for those instances when your team isn't sure it will control the tip but is willing to gamble for the steal. The small forward and the strong forward anticipate that the tip will go to the outside; the moment the ball is touched, they try to beat the opposition to it. Since the opposition rarely anticipates this kind of aggressiveness, the play stands a reasonable chance of working. If it doesn't work, however, the point guard is positioned at the top of the defensive key to slow the opposition's offensive attack.

OUT-OF-BOUNDS PLAYS

During play, balls do go out of bounds, both under the basket and along the sidelines. Many times, inexperienced offenses don't know how to bring the ball inbounds without it being stolen away. The following plays are designed to correct that problem so that other teams *never* steal the ball from your team on any out-of-bounds play.

An Out-of-Bounds Play from Under the Basket

In this play, the point guard, standing to the left of the basket and underneath it, is responsible for putting the ball into play. Remember, once he receives the ball from the referee, he has five seconds in which to do his job.

The other four players are in a box formation at the four corners of the key. The moment the point guard receives the ball and slaps it, the center, posted low and in front of the point guard, cuts across the lane and picks for the small forward who is stationed across from him. Meanwhile, the strong forward, posted high on the point guard's side of the key, sets a similar pick for the shooting guard at the

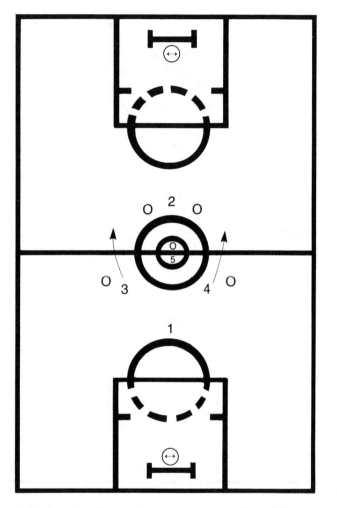

A Defensive Formation   O = Offense

Out-of-Bounds Play

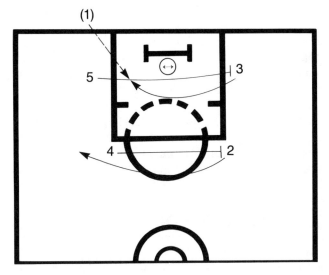

Baseline Option #1

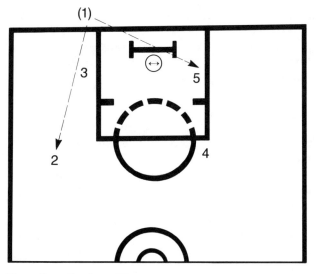

Baseline Option #2

top of the circle. *The point guard's first option is to pass to the small forward.*

If the small forward is not open for the ball, the point guard looks for the center who turns toward the ball after setting the pick for the small forward. If neither of these two players is open, the point guard looks to the top of the key for the shooting guard as an outlet.

Every player's movement throughout this out-of-bounds play should be quick and smooth, and the point guard's first objective should be to pass the ball inbounds to a player who has an easy shot (in this case, the small forward). Indeed, the inbounding team's first objective should be to score an easy basket. But if that is not possible, the next most important objective is to pass the ball safely inbounds before five seconds elapses.

An Out-of-Bounds Play from the Sidelines

In this play, the strong forward takes the ball out-of-bounds. The point guard and the shooting guard are posted low on either side of the basket, and the center and small forward are posted high to complete the box formation. At the slap of the ball, the center goes down to the low post on his side and sets a pick for the point guard, giving the strong forward two options: 1) He can pass the ball to the point guard, who moves upcourt off the pick, or 2) he can pass to the center who, after setting the pick, turns and looks for the ball.

If the point guard receives the ball, he immediately looks to the weak side of the court for the shooting guard. At the moment the pass was put inbounds, the small forward set a pick for the shooting guard near the low post. The shooting guard has cut from the outside of the pick toward the corner of the foul line and is in good position for an easy jump shot. But if, for some reason, the shooting guard is guarded, or if there is a mismatch on the pick that freed him, the point guard can also look for the small forward since he is even closer to the basket.

Unless a team simply wants to run out the clock, an out-of-bounds play should always be regarded as a scoring opportunity. There are numerous other out-of-bounds plays, some which stack the four of-

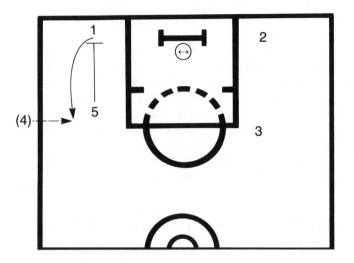

Sideline Option #1

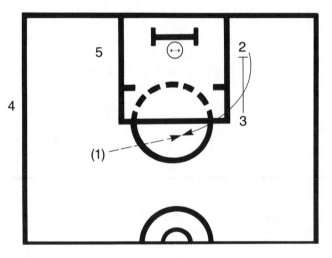

Sideline Option #2

fensive men along one side of the key, others which form a line across the court, but I like the plays I've shown you because 1) they're simple, 2) they keep the court balanced, 3) they open more than one player for a good shot, 4) they work! Whatever your role in an out-of-bounds play—as passer, pick-setter, or receiver—it's important not to let yourself become intimidated by the defense. You and your teammates have a play, which puts you at a distinct advantage over the defense who don't know what you'll do next. Why undermine that advantage by allowing an aggressive defender to get on your case? Instead, remember your role, move precisely—and if you're the passer, give your teammate your very best pass, perhaps faking a different pass first and then passing, so that the out-of-bounds play is a success.

LAST-SECOND OFFENSES

Last-second offenses have become an extremely important part of today's game. In high school and college basketball, a last-second offense can be used to take the last shot at the quarter (high school), or the half (college). Pro teams use such offenses in the final seconds of each quarter in order to have two shots to their opponent's one. At any level—high school, college, or pro—the last-second offense is designed usually to take advantage of an opponent's defense.

College Ball

Most of the time, college teams call a last-second offense just before the half or at the end of the game. As half-time approaches, the strategy is to hold the ball for a good shot just before the final buzzer sounds keeping in mind the 45 second clock. That means that the offensive team usually needs to run some kind of delaying offense until the final seconds of the half. Against a man-to-man defense, the delay might take the form of a passing game with lots of off-the-ball movement, or it can be a 1-4 set with the point guard holding the ball until there are eight to ten seconds on the clock before making his move.

Against a zone defense, the offense can still hold the ball out front, but it must allow itself more time—ten to fifteen seconds—to work the ball around and move the defense in order to get a good shot.

This method for dealing with zones applies equally well to high school play. It's important at both levels to get a shot up with about four seconds left so that there is a chance for a tip-in or an offensive rebound.

High School Ball

The difference between high school and college basketball is that high schoolers play eight minute quarters rather than twenty minute halves, so it's critical for a high school team to know the time and situation with less than two minutes to play in a given quarter.

A good way for high school teams to practice last-second offenses is for the coach to give them situations in practice. "The game is tied and there are twenty seconds left in the game. What do you do?" "You're down by one point and have fifteen seconds to get off a good shot. Who should take it? Where?" etc. Skull sessions such as these get an entire team thinking as a unit, and often the situations are far more complex than they at first appear. Let's look at an example.

Say your team has a one-point lead and there are thirty seconds left in the game. Your team has just grabbed the defensive rebound. What should you do?

First, unless there is a 100 percent chance of completing a baseball pass for a successful fast break, hold the ball. You don't want to give the ball away to the opposition.

Second, give the ball to your best ballhandler so that he can move the ball up the court. Again, you want to minimize the risk of a turnover. If your best ballhandler also happens to be your best foul-shooter, or one of the best, all the better. The defense might foul intentionally right away, in which case you want your best foul shooter on the line.

Third, make sure your offense spreads the defense so if there is any double-teaming it's readily apparent and your players can pass to the free man for an easy basket.

Fourth, avoid long lobs and cross-court passes. Short, crisp passes and lots of off-the-ball movement are the norm in this situation; certainly no one on offense should be standing around—that just makes the defense's job easier.

Situations like the above are common at every

level of basketball. If a team wants to preserve a close lead or pull out a win in a game's final seconds, it must understand all its options and the complexities that each last-minute situation presents. It's a heartbreaking shame to see a team blow a lead or miss a go-ahead basket in the final seconds of a game because it didn't know what it was doing.

Pro Ball

Pro teams use the same last-second strategies as high school teams, especially in the first three quarters. The only variable affecting the pros' strategy is the 24-second shot rule; pro teams must shoot the ball within 24 seconds or turn the ball over to the other team.

The 24-second rule quickens the pace of a pro team's strategy as the end of a quarter nears. Pro teams usually try to get off two shots to their opponents' one before the buzzer sounds, and this requires keeping close track of the seconds left in the quarter. Normally, pro teams will try to get a shot off with 36 seconds left and then play all-out defense. If the opposition takes the full 24 seconds to get off its shot, there are still 12 seconds left on the clock, and 12 seconds, as any pro will tell you, is ample time to move the ball upcourt and get off a good shot before the quarter ends.

The biggest difference in last-second strategy between the pros and other levels is the pros' approach to the closing moments of the game. In the pro game's last two minutes, the clock is stopped after every basket, and if a time-out is called in the backcourt, the ball can be put inbounds from midcourt if the coach desires. This latter rule has helped many a pro team win a game in its closing seconds.

No matter what the level of basketball, last-second offenses are nothing but specific responses to game situations. Teams must review as many situations as they can during practice, so that when they face them in a game, in the heat of excitement, they know in advance what to do.

During practice, coaches should treat last-second situations as opportunities for communication between them and their players. Players should be encouraged to voice the options a situation presents as they see them; verbal participation keeps every player involved. Moreover, coaches should present last-second situations at every practice. Reason? No two situations are identical and teams must become adept at responding instantaneously to the options each situation presents. The rewards of such practice are several. Not only will a team play well under the pressure of a last-second situation, it will also come to trust the coach's strategy and learn to think as a team.

THE TEN WORST OFFENSIVE HABITS TO WATCH FOR

Nobody's perfect, but the complete player strives to be as close to perfection as possible. Through the years I've seen many bad habits repeated on offense, each one the opposite of perfection. Each one gives coaches gray hair, but worse, if you're guilty of any of them, they hinder your development and sap your natural playing skills. What follows is a list of ten of the worst habits an offensive player can be guilty of. If any of these habits are part of your game, make every effort to rid yourself of them. You'll be doing yourself—and your team—a big favor.

THE TEN WORST OFFENSIVE HABITS

1. Too much one-on-one.
2. Too much standing around and watching your teammates.
3. Thinking "shot" before thinking "pass." Always be aware of both and of your teammates' presence on the floor and the defense's actions.
4. Not looking for more than one option on a set play.
5. Telegraphing passes which the defense can steal.
6. Overcompensating for a mistake by committing an immediate, foolish foul.
7. Faking out your teammates with new and creative fakes that they're not familiar with.
8. Not being aware of how much time is left on the clock toward the end of a quarter, half; toward the end of the game.
9. Losing your concentration.
10. Not making your cuts and moves at game speed during a set play.

7

Team Defense

Late in my career, I had the great good fortune to play for Red Holzman, one of the finest strategists ever to coach in the NBA. Red is an uncanny judge of basketball talent, as I witnessed in numerous late-game situations when he rotated players on and off the floor to capitalize on their offensive or defensive prowess. Red's special talent as a coach is teaching defense; indeed, no other coach in the NBA knows as much on the subject as he. Many basketball experts feel that the two New York Knicks teams that Red coached to NBA Championships in 1969-70 and 1972-73 were able to win primarily because they were great defensive clubs, capable of turning back even the most blistering offensive attacks.

Later, when I became an assistant coach under Red, I learned what a coaching genius he really was. I saw that, while many coaches were content to develop team offenses and let their defenses more or less take care of themselves, Red felt that a team without a solid, consistent team defense was really only half a team, at the mercy of their own scoring percentage and the overall strengths of the opposition. He and I would scout college prospects, and what Red taught me to look for defensively in a player were ten important characteristics. I want to pass those characteristics on to you and then show you how you and your teammates can play better defensive basketball. We'll also go into the intricacies of the man-to-man and various zone defenses, with a close look at the advantages and disadvantages of each.

Red Holzman used to say that a coach is only as good as his players are. The same holds true for a team. The player who can't play intelligent defense is ultimately a hindrance to a team and an embarrassment to his coach. Fortunately, there are ways that you as an individual can work on your defense to avoid these shortcomings, and the best place to start is by measuring your defensive abilities against Red Holzman's ten criteria. As you read on, keep in mind the old adage: "If your opponent does not score, he cannot win." Of course, in basketball, opponents do score, but there are ways, both individually and as a team, that you and your teammates can limit an opposition's scoring potential so that your team can score more points and win, and it's the purpose of this chapter to show you how.

For now, let's see how you rate defensively.

Red Holzman's List of Ten Criteria for Determining Whether or Not *You* Are a Complete Defensive Player

1. *Do you have quick hands and feet?* Quickness is a must on defense where a split-second can make the difference between a blocked shot and a score.
2. *Do you have long arms?* Players with longer arms have an advantage on defense (and offense, too) over their shorter-armed teammates.
3. *Are you a quick jumper?* The best shot-blockers and rebounders can launch themselves off the floor in an instant—and keep jumping as long as necessary.

4. *Is your coach defense minded?* You'll know that he is if he spends more time coaching you and your team on defense than he does on offense. If he's not defense minded, your team is in trouble, especially on those nights when the ball is not going into the basket as frequently as you'd like. Defense, and only defense will win those games.

5. *Do you know a variety of defenses?* Do you know how to play man-to-man defense? Zone defenses such as the 2-3? the 2-1-2? Do you know how to apply the full-court press? The half-court press? If you do, count yourself a student of defense. If you don't, read on and learn.

6. *How good are you at making the transition from offense to defense?* Do you tend to be the last person up the floor? Is the man you're assigned to guard always beating you on the fast break? These are just two signs that your transition game from offense to defense needs serious work.

7. *How intelligent are you as a player?* Do you feel you understand the concepts behind basketball and how it's played? Articulate those concepts to yourself. In a game, do you feel you play under control and understand the situation that each moment in the game presents? Do you possess total player vision—that is, the ability to see and understand everything that's happening on the floor?

8. *Do you talk on defense?* Not about homework or girlfriends. Do you talk to your teammates about what's happening in the game? Do you warn them about possible picks the opposition is setting? Do you yell "Switch!" before you switch men with a teammate defensively? Do you yell encouragements to your teammates and yourself? Red Holzman knows that the player who talks on defense is the one he can count on always to have his head in a game.

9. *Do you know how to position yourself so that you can see the ball on the weak side?* If you don't know what I'm talking about, read on and I'll show you.

10. *Do you practice the proper defensive stance when playing defense?* What is the proper defensive stance? You'd better read on just to make sure you both know it, and can do it!

These are ten of Red Holzman's criteria for evaluating a player's defensive qualities. There are others, but as Red used to say to me when we'd talk defense into the night, if a player can honestly answer "Yes" to all ten of the above, then everyone—player, coach, and team—will look terrific. "If a player's ever going to be good—offensively or defensively—" Red always said, "he's eventually got to study basketball the way he studies any subject in school."

We've got a lot of things to study about defense. Let's get started.

PLAYING AGGRESSIVE DEFENSE

Not all players can score consistently, but everyone on defense should be able to carry his load and perform equally well.

In basketball, there are two kinds of defense: *man-to-man,* where each defensive player guards an individual opponent whenever the opposition controls the ball, and *zone defense,* where each player covers a different territory (usually in the area surrounding the basket) and tries to prevent the opposition from penetrating with the ball into that territory. More so than any other phase of basketball, there is only one way that either defense can work, and that's when every defender plays aggressively. Good defensive teams can keep pressure on the ball at will, and they achieve this ability by always playing as aggressively as they can. That doesn't mean they stop thinking on defense and turn into animals and make mistakes and foul unnecessarily. It means they're playing fierce, tough scrappy defense, and the morale of each player is so high that nothing can shake their unity of purpose. Aggressive defense demands from every individual hard work, alertness, determination, and pride. Needless to say, defense is no place to loaf. There's an old basketball cliche: "If you want to rest, rest on offense, not defense." Let's not plan to rest during any phase of our game if we're calling ourselves complete players, but let's certainly not rest on defense.

The Proper Defensive Stances

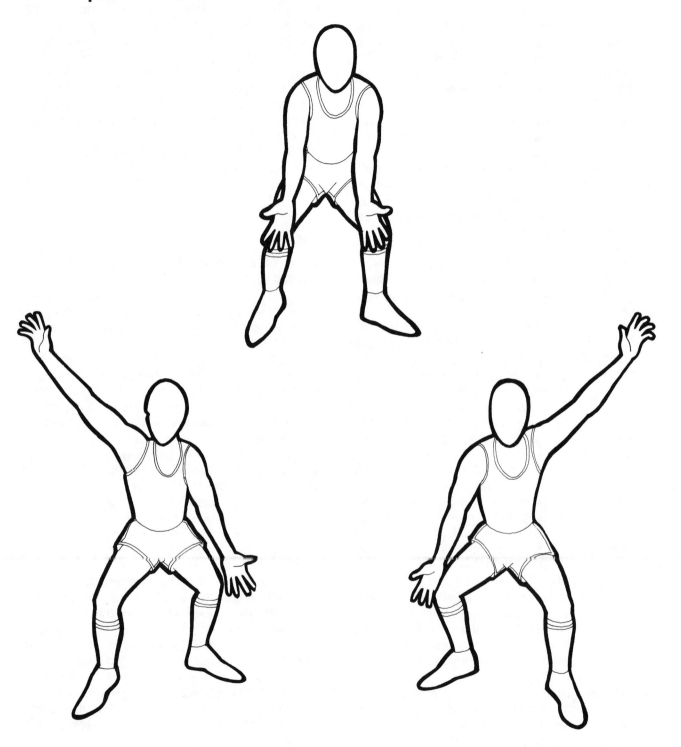

THE THREE QUALITIES OF A SUCCESSFUL AGGRESSIVE DEFENSE

Aggressive defenses are successful for many reasons, but each shares three important qualities that feed and nurture its aggressiveness, and thus its success. There are qualities that you can instill in yourself as one-fifth of your team's defense. If your teammates can do the same, watch out—your team is on its way to defensive greatness.

1. *The successful aggressive defensive team is well-conditioned*—everyone on the team can play to his fullest for an entire game. Superior conditioning does not just happen. It requires a planned conditioning program and a commitment from every player to become physically fit. The best-conditioned players participate in year-round conditioning programs. See my next chapter on tailoring a year-round program to meet your goals.

2. *Both the coach and his players must be sold on the defense.* The coach must explain clearly to his players the merits of the defense he wishes them to use, and the players must unite behind a common individual and team pride to make that defense work!

3. *Each individual player must be dedicated, loyal, and hardworking.* If you're ever going to play quality defense, you must be a real competitor who continually strives to outhustle, outmaneuver, outsmart, and outplay your opponent. The aggressive defensive player is like a taut coil, always ready to spring after a pass or loose ball, cut off a loose man, stop the dribbler, or otherwise do everything legal within his power to prevent offensive penetration. Furthermore, the complete defensive player knows how to exploit his opponent's weaknesses.

Team spirit is the key to successful team defense. Each player must be willing to work, not just for himself, but for the team. As we'll see, defense requires less sophisticated talents than offense, so there's really no excuse for any player not to do an adequate defensive job. Keep notes on your defensive strengths and weaknesses and those of your team. Work hard to maintain the strengths, but seek to eliminate the weaknesses.

MAN-TO-MAN DEFENSE

There are three facets to the man-to-man defense: 1) containing the offense (that is, frustrating, or even preventing its attempt to move the ball toward the basket), 2) channeling the dribbler toward a trap (more on this shortly), and 3) guarding the dribbler individually. Each facet has a place in the team's total defense, and when used interchangeably, each can keep an offense confused, guessing, and off-balance. Let's look at each facet.

Containment

When playing a containing man-to-man defense, each defensive player is responsible for keeping his opponent in front of him. If you're called on to play man-to-man, you must at all times try to stay low, keep your knees bent, your feet spread slightly apart, and your body balanced in a stance akin to a boxer's. When defensing a dribbler, concentrate on the dribbler's hips. A dribbler can fake with the ball, with his feet, head, or shoulders, but he cannot move where he wants to go without moving his hips. By concentrating on his hips, you can stay with the dribbler, no matter what fakes he throws at you.

In general, when playing man-to-man defense, try to stay close to your opponent but don't gamble by letting him get between you and the basket. If your opponent is on the weak side of the court (the side opposite from where the ball is), you must position yourself so that you can see both him and the ball. In basketball, this is known as "opening up."

There is normally no switching off in containment defense. Each player is responsible for his or her own opponent. The only time you should switch is when you (or your teammate) are the victim of a good offensive pick and the switch is essential to maintain coverage of the dribbler. And yet, if everyone on the team plays alert, there should be no need even for this exception to the rule.

When playing a containment defense, there are a number of questions every defensive player should ask himself. First, how quick is the player I'm guarding? Should I back off a half step so he can't pass me and penetrate the defense? Is his off-the-ball movement good or does he stand around a lot? If you know your opponent's strengths and weaknesses, you'll always be one step ahead of him on the court.

The last big key, which coaches must teach and players must practice in order to play a solid, successful containment man-to-man defense is *communication*. Even when an offensive player beats his opponent, a team can prevent him from getting off an uncontested shot if the appropriate defensive players can switch off quickly enough, and the way they effect the switch is by communicating with each other. Coaches should make certain their players all use the same terminology when communicating on defense, and every player should know precisely what teammates mean by shouts of "Pick right!" "Pick left!" "Switch!" "Stay!" "I've got 45!" etc.

Channeling the Dribbler to the Trap

A trap is a defensive play wherein the dribbler suddenly finds himself heavily double-teamed and with no room to move. It involves a defensive player called the *container* channeling the dribbler in the direction of a second defender called the *trapper* and the two defenders making movement for the dribbler impossible. To channel a dribbler properly, assume your guarding stance a half step to the side opposite the direction you want the dribbler to move. If you want to channel him to your left, play him a half step to the right; if you want to channel him to the right, vice versa. This is called *overplaying* your man, and you want to be so positioned that you can still contain him in case the trap fails to develop. Stay low, keep your knees bent, your feet a shoulder's width apart, your body balanced, and move sideways by sliding your feet together and then apart so that the dribbler cannot change direction. Ideally, if you're overplaying him well, you'll lull the dribbler into feeling he's moving in a direction he wants to go.

As you move the dribbler toward the spot on the floor where you hope to trap him (and most traps occur near the sidelines or the corners so that the dribbler cannot turn away from his defenders without going out of bounds), keep your hands and eyes busy. Jab at the ball—don't lunge for it—with your outside hand while maintaining your proper balance and defensive stance. Never allow the dribbler to

The Best Areas to Trap

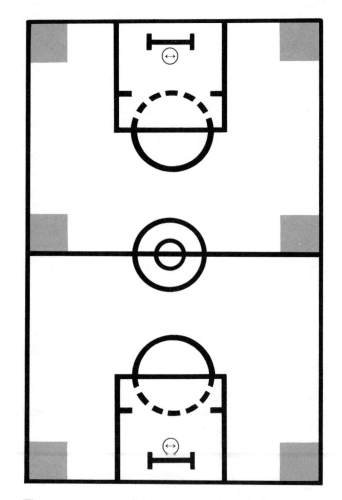

The most successful traps take place in the corners or along the sideline before the midcourt line.

advance vertically without harassing him. Keep your eyes open for your teammate (the trapper in the play), coming to assist you. Normally, you want to trap the man within a three-foot area anywhere along the sideline, although sometimes, depending upon his and your quickness, you may need to give him more room. As the dribbler approaches the spot near the sideline, the trapper leaves his man and runs directly at the dribbler, waving his arms. If the trap works and you and your teammate succeed in trapping the dribbler who looks for a free man to pass to, then you and your teammate stand a good chance of stealing the ball, forcing a turnover, or at least forcing a jump ball.

The trapper must be on the alert as he moves in to make the trap for the possibility of the dribbler cutting around him or reversing direction. However, if the trapper has timed his move properly, the dribbler will become flustered and yield the ball. *Any trap which results in a steal and quick basket should be followed by another trap.* This creates a frenzied atmosphere in which unpoised ballhandlers always succumb. Watch, too, for moments when the dribbler turns his back on you; these are excellent times to trap or at least double-team him.

Defensing the Dribbler Individually

Keeping your hands busy is essential during any phase of defense, particularly when you're guarding the dribbler man-to-man. The best defensive players harass their opponents with a constant flurry of hand movements. When going one-on-one against a dribbler, always poke, chop, jab at the ball, wave your hands in the dribbler's face; in general make a nuisance of yourself. If the dribbler has a favorite dribbling hand—and 99 percent of all dribblers do—overplay him to that side so that you force him either to switch hands or stop dribbling. Maintaining proper body position is critical here, but most important is concentrating on the dribbler's hips so that he can't throw a successful fake at you with another part of his body and break free.

Your hands should be up and moving at all times, and if the ballhandler suddenly goes up for a shot, you should jump straight up with him and try to deflect the shot without touching the shooter at all. Just brushing the bottom of the ball with your fingertips can be enough to sufficiently block the shot.

It takes a special alertness to avoid being faked on the vertical jump, and blocking shots in heavy traffic under the boards is never easy. But with practice, shot-blocking can be learned (see Chapter 4, The Backboard Drill), and it's a skill you can apply as well when playing in a zone. In all, it's worth remembering that one cleanly-blocked shot can intimidate the opposition and perhaps even make the difference in the game.

Overplaying the Pass

Besides overplaying the dribbler—that is, forcing him to switch hands, move in a certain direction, or stop—smart man-to-man defensive players also know how to overplay the pass. In basketball terminology, this is known as "playing the passing lanes," and it involves positioning yourself in such a way against your opponent when he does not have the ball that you can deflect a chest pass to him, intercept a bounce pass, prevent him from going to a favorite spot on the floor, or "open up" to see the ball in order to prevent a back-door cut. When overplaying the pass, keep your weight on your back foot so that you can push off of it to steal a pass, but try to stay balanced and never lean forward lest you make yourself vulnerable to the back-door cut.

When overplaying a prospective passer, keep pressure on him so that he can't make an easy pass to a teammate. In general overplaying involves a certain risk in the hope of forcing turnovers. If you don't pressure the ballhandler, he'll eventually beat you, and your teammates won't have time to switch off or help you. Never give an opponent an easy pass; make him earn it.

Switching

Switching men with a teammate in the middle of a man-to-man defense requires clear communication between the two of you. As we saw in the previous chapter on team offense, a dribbler will frequently try to shake free of his defender by running the man into one of his own teammates who stands in the defender's way (sets a pick). The dribbler then can either dribble around both men for an easy shot, or pass to his picking man who might roll away from the pick toward the basket (the pick and roll). Both moves can be effective, but there are methods for you and your defense to beat the pick so long as you all play alertly and communicate out loud with each other. Each method involves switching men with a teammate, and there are three ways to switch effectively:

1. When you're defensing the dribbler, you can come right to the point of the pick and then switch men with your teammate who, up until then, has been guarding the picker.

2. Your teammate can run between you and the picker and "show himself" to stop the dribbler, aggressively yelling "Switch!" and staying with the dribbler while you slide behind the picker and defense him.

3. You and your teammates can (and should) agree to switch automatically on any pick twenty feet or closer to the basket.

Some players feel they've failed somehow if they have to switch men with a teammate, but switching is nothing to be ashamed of. Rather, it's the best solution to an otherwise harmful offensive play. *No switch should ever be subtle.* If you're taking the dribbler on in the switch, step right up to him and show yourself and bellow "Switch!" Don't let him cut past you, but don't overcompensate for that possibilty by switching with your teammate from too far away. You run the risk of leaving both the dribbler and the picker unguarded.

I like to see a man assigned to the dribbler switching with his teammate when he's closest to the pick (option #1 above). The move gives the two defenders the option of double-teaming the dribbler, which is something they can't do if they start the switch from too far away.

Man-to-man defense, played well, is a tremendous motivator as players try to stop their men from doing significant damage on offense. I know from my own playing days that one of a player's sweetest moments is when he can look at a box score and see that he's held his man nearly scoreless. Sure, there are dangers to playing man-to-man defense; defenders tend to foul more than they do when playing zone defense, and a poorly-conditioned defense can literally be run off the floor. But the man-to-man allows coaches to make adjustments easily and as-sign their players to the men they're most capable of guarding, and players profit enormously from having to stick to their men like glue. Nothing is more intrinsic in basketball than these one-on-one match-ups. Man-to-man defense is basketball played at its roots.

ZONE DEFENSES

Zone defenses are being played more and more at the high school and college levels. Even in the professional ranks teams like the New York Knicks and Milwaukee Bucks use zone principles to apply pressure on their opponents and alter the tempo of a game.

There are numerous zone defenses today, and, when played properly by a team, they can frustrate even the best shooting and ballhandling teams.

Many critics call the zone the "lazy man's defense," but this is a total misnomer. Playing zones well requires concentration, communication, good footwork, excellent lateral movement, proper body position and conditioning—all the things required to play man-to-man defense well.

Why do teams play a zone defense? There are numerous answers to this question. First, a team may not be quick enough to play man-to-man defense against certain teams, or it may want to confuse an opponent and force it to take a perimeter shot (most zone defenses make penetrating toward the basket difficult). Sometimes teams will go into a zone when a key player (or players) is in foul trouble, or when it wants to position itself better for defensive rebounds. These and other circumstances can govern coaches' choice of the zone.

The chief zones in use today are the 2-1-2, the 1-3-1, the 2-3, and several pressing zones, including the 2-2-1 zone press and the 1-3-1 halfcourt press. Let's look at them all.

The 2-1-2 Zone

Of all the zone defenses in use today, the 2-1-2 is probably the most common. Its purpose is to cover the entire potential scoring area well, rather than

The 2-1-2 Zone Formation

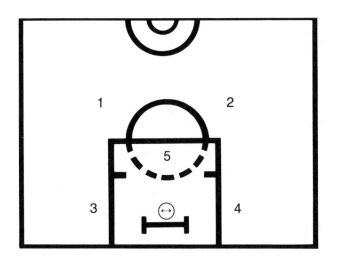

concentrate manpower in one particular area to the detriment of the whole. It allows teams that use it to cover the foul-line area well, start fast breaks easily, box out on rebounds, stymie teams that rely on working inside, and thwart all off-the-ball offensive penetration.

Its weaknesses are that it's sometimes difficult for the team using it to cover shots from the outside and the corners, and it's particularly vulnerable to shots from the baseline and the top of the key.

Some college and high school coaches are using the 2-1-2 as a kind of match-up zone when the opposition has a prolific scorer. In this form of the 2-1-2, a defender plays the prolific scorer man-to-man whenever he enters his zone, and he calls to the appropriate teammate to pick the man up when the man leaves the zone for a new one. In this way, a team can keep track of a scorer at all times, control his attack, and still maintain a unified defense with all the advantages listed above. It takes practice, discipline, and total team communication to make the 2-1-2 work as a match-up zone, but the rewards are well worth the effort.

The 1-3-1 Zone

The 1-3-1 zone defense is extremely effective in forcing the perimeter shot. It requires a player with great quickness to play at the top of the key, and a player with great quickness, anticipation, and corner-to-corner baseline covering ability to play the bottom of the key.

The 1-3-1 allows strong coverage in the foul-line area, neutralizes the three-man overloading style so often seen today, cripples any high- or low-post offenses, forces considerable offensive adjustment, and covers most of the dangerous jump shot areas.

Its weaknesses? It leaves a defense very vulnerable to good corner shooters, it does not cover the rebounding area as well as other zones, it yields carefully executed short baseline jump shots, it does not complement a fast-break offense very well, and it tends to wear down its wing men.

Still, the 1-3-1's imbalance makes it difficult for offenses to match it suitably, and it puts the man at the top of the key and either of the wing men in perfect position for executing a half-court trap. In all, teams that use the 1-3-1 must possess a high degree of court sophistication and stamina.

The 1-3-1 Zone Formation

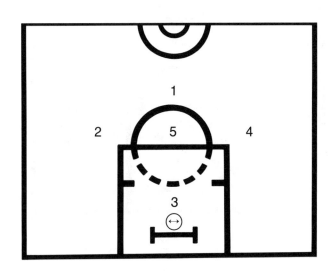

The 2-3 Zone

The 2-3 zone defense is generally regarded as the first effective zone defense ever used. From it emerged the 2-1-2: the middle man moved forward from the back line and the two front players moved closer together.

The 2-3's strengths are several. As you can see from studying the diagram, it allows good coverage against the easy lay-up, the set shot, and corner and baseline shots, and it puts big players in perfect position for the defensive rebound. In addition, it complements a team's fast break or transition game, and can effectively stifle offensive teams that like to post low.

Although the 2-3 is considered the first effective zone defense, it is vulnerable to shots near the foul-line and high post areas, and offenses can easily overload one side of the court to move the zone in that direction, and then, with a swift pass, get off a clean shot on the weak side. In general, strong jump-shooting teams have good success against the 2-3, as do those that penetrate the middle, between the 2-3's two lines.

The 2-3 Zone Formation

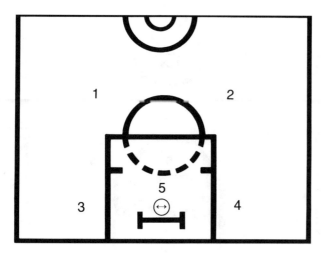

Variations of the above zones include the 2-3, the 1-2-2, and the 2-2-1, also known as the Box and One. In this latter zone, a single player is often assigned to defense an opposition's top shooter while his teammates cover the key in a 2-2 box. As you can see from looking at the 2-1-2, the 1-3-1 and the 2-3, each lends itself to different configurations depending upon the defensive needs of the moment (the 2-3 can easily convert to the 2-1-2, the 1-3-1 can easily convert to the Box-and-One, etc.). It's up to a coach to know which zone defense is best for his personnel and what shots he wants his opponents to take. No zone is easy to play and only regular practice and constant communication between players can make it work.

PRESSING DEFENSES

Any pressing defense is a kind of gamble normally used to force turnovers and get a team back into a game. Presses can also serve 1) to keep the ball-control team from controlling the tempo of a game, 2) to overwhelm slow teams and poor ballhandlers, 3) to rattle inexperienced teams into making many errors, 4) to force an upcoming opponent to spend valuable practice time preparing for it. Pressing defenses have a wonderful way of bringing out a team's aggressiveness, and practiced properly and executed well, they always instill in their practitioners a unified, positive attitude.

Presses do have their drawbacks. For one, they require of a team great stamina, quickness, aggressiveness, and anticipation, and, since they spread a defense all over the floor, every man must do his job or else find himself giving up the easy basket or fouling unnecessarily. In addition, there are so many variables to consider when practicing a press—particularly how the offense will respond to it—that players can easily become discouraged and a team's morale can suffer.

Therefore, if your coach decides to install a press, whether a man-to-man or one of several zones, be prepared to work hard. But know that if your team can master a press—in short, if every individual does his job—it has added immeasurably to its defensive capabilities, and opponents will no longer be able to take your defense for granted.

The 2-2-1 Zone Press

The 2-2-1 is chiefly employed either *to slow an opponent's offensive flow* or *to force turnovers.* When used for slowing an offense after a basket or a free throw has been made, it involves defensive players matching themselves against the opposition players in front of them. Normally, this means that the defense's guards cover the two men bringing up the ball, the forwards cover the men to either side of the court, and the center serves as a safety valve near the defensive goal in case the opposition slips past the first two lines of defense. The center's role in this press is particularly vital; since he can see the entire court, his job includes shouting information to his teammates who can't see what's happening behind them.

When the purpose of the press is to slow the opposition's offense, matching up should occur as soon as the ball goes to the offense. This is relatively easy to do after a free throw has been made—the opposition is divided evenly on either side of the key. But after a basket, there can be confusion, and the only way at times to prevent the press from being broken before it's even formed is for teammates to talk to each other and perhaps even switch off.

To play the 2-2-1 zone press for turnovers, a defense must play aggressively; a guard must put man-to-man pressure on the dribbler and force him to the outside toward either of the forwards. This is when knowing how to overplay a dribbler becomes vital, lest he break the defense with a pass or a change of direction.

The guard moves the dribbler toward a forward in order to trap the dribbler. As was true in the man-to-man trap discussed earlier, the best place to trap the dribbler is either down the sideline or in the corner, and even if the dribbler manages to pass the ball past the first line of defense, the ball can still be double-teamed (by a forward and the center), especially if the pass is made downcourt into the corner.

The 2-2-1 normally turns into a 2-1-2 formation —that is, the center moves up to the middle of the key and the forwards drop down to the baseline—if an opponent tries to break the original formation. If an opponent tries to take advantage of the 2-2-1's weak middle by putting a player there, the best ad-

The 2-2-1 Zone Press (Full Court)

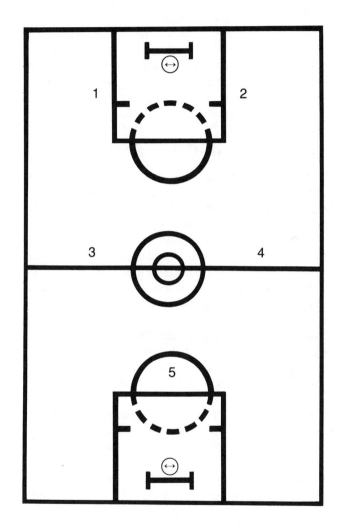

justment is to put a guard or forward on him.

Whether your team uses the 2-2-1 zone press to slow an opponent's offense or to force turnovers, it always runs the risk of being broken, especially if you and your teammates fail to communicate with each other. No doubt your coach in practice will want to walk you through the numerous different trapping options that the 2-2-1 presents, and show you how the defense rotates in the direction of the ball. Red Holzman is absolutely right when he says that a player should study basketball the same way he studies his school subjects. Such an approach is essential when learning defensive zones, especially one as demanding as the 2-2-1 zone press.

The 1-3-1 Half-Court Press

The 1-3-1 half-court press can be very effective in upsetting the tempo of your opponent and can also give your team a better chance for rebounds if the opposition settles for the perimeter shot.

Once again, the player at the point of the 1-3-1 must try to force the dribbler down either side of the court where he can be trapped along the sideline or in the corner by either of the two wing men. Once the trap is under way, the other three defenders are responsible for guarding the baseline, the key, and the weak side. They do that by maintaining solid defensive form (body low, knees bent, back straight, feet spread, hands up and moving), exceptional alertness, and above all, constant communication with each other.

Besides being geared for the trap, the 1-3-1 is also a beautiful formation for intercepting cross-court or bounce passes, which desperate dribblers often tend to try. Again, as with the 2-2-1, learning the 1-3-1 takes time, lots of it, and patience, more patience than some players think they have. During practice, you may become frustrated from repeatedly having to walk through these formations. What's all this for, you may wonder? Why can't we just practice and play?

The 1-3-1 Half-Court Press

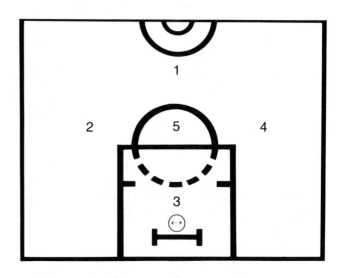

Be patient. Basketball is never that simple. Your coach has a plan for the team, and you and your teammates can make it work. You're looking for turnovers. You're trying to slow an opposition's offense. You want to prevent them from scoring. You want to be optimally positioned for grabbing the defensive rebound. All of that takes practice and an array of defensive formations.

Now get in there. Get your head back into practice and understand precisely what the coach wants you to do: namely, play defense as a team. By knowing how to play these formations, you ultimately should be able to stop any offense in its tracks. *That's* what all the practice is for, and that's why you must never allow frustration to enter your game.

And when you hear the crowd—your crowd—out of love and admiration shouting "DEE-FENSE! DEE-FENSE!" you'll know that you and your team have finally arrived. Why? Because when all is said and done, *no team is better than its defense.*

8

Conditioning

Basketball is a physically demanding sport, and playing it well requires that your body (and mind and soul) be in top shape. That means a correctly-tailored year-round conditioning program, first, to build, and then to maintain your strength, speed, power, and endurance. I have always found conditioning for basketball essential for three reasons: first, proper conditioning reduces the possibility and lessens the severity of serious injury. Second, proper conditioning can give you a significant advantage over a less-conditioned opponent. Third, being properly conditioned can help you play to your maximum potential, which, after all, is what the complete player strives for.

The purpose of this chapter is to provide you with a well-rounded conditioning program for basketball. As with anything else worth doing, you'll get out of it exactly what you put in—there are no shortcuts to making it work for you. But if you supply the necessary discipline and desire, the program will reward you many times over with the physical tools for improving your overall game.

Incidentally, before embarking on *any* conditioning program, you *should* first always receive a complete medical check-up from a licensed physician. Conditioning for basketball is strenuous business; you want to be absolutely certain there is nothing wrong with your body before putting it under the stress of hard exercise.

THE COMPLETE BASKETBALL PLAYER'S CONCISE CONDITIONING AND BODY CARE PROGRAM

The following program, divided between an in-season and an off-season schedule, is designed to keep you fit for basketball all year-round. As you'll see, the off-season program is tailored to help you build strength, stamina, speed, and power in preparation for the actual season, while the in-season program is meant to help you maintain all those off-season gains. Serious basketball players recognize that their training schedule revolves around this cycle of conditioning and maintenance. Since you're young and growing, there's no reason why you can't think of the cycle as an ascending spiral; in other words, every year on the program should make you even better conditioned to play the game.

Specifics

Besides having an in-season and an off-season schedule, every training cycle for any sport also includes a period of rest. For basketball, sports physiologists recommend a lay-off period of about one month, usually taken at the end of the regular playing season. This lay-off serves to give the body time to heal and rejuvenate itself after all the physical stress it's undergone, and it also ensures that the player doesn't get bored with the game. Sports psychologists tell us that athletes can suffer cases of the much-dreaded burn-out just as readily as overworked businessmen. It's important to remember, then, that you play and train for basketball because you love the game, and therefore you should not make a job of it. Instead, relax during the first month of the off-season and forget basketball. Go to the movies, ride your bicycle, watch TV, visit your friends, read—in short, be kind to yourself. Then, once the period of your off-season training begins,

start slowly with the program, gradually increasing the numbers of repetitions (and in the case of your weight program, gradually increasing weight) so that your most intensive off-season conditioning occurs through the summer and early fall. Thereafter, you should slack off somewhat on the off-season conditioning program and start working more on individual basketball drills (see Chapter 3) to help improve your shooting, passing, and dribbling. And throughout the basketball season itself, you should follow the in-season program shown on page 106 to help you maintain what you've gained.

If you were to chart a twelve-month training cycle for basketball, it might look like this:

Month 1

Off-season; rest and relaxation.

Month 2

Off-season conditioning program begins.

Month 3

Off-season conditioning program intensifies. More sets, more weights, more repetitions, distances.

Month 4

Off-season conditioning program peaks. Maximum sets, weight, repetitions, distances.

Month 5

Taper-off period. Reduce all off-season conditioning. Begin practicing individual basketball drills.

Month 6

Minimal off-season conditioning. Intensive pre-season personal and team basketball practice.

Months 7–11

Begin in-season conditioning program.

Month 12

Taper off: post-season.

Notice how the off-season conditioning program builds gradually, peaks in month four, then tapers off. The reason for this tapering-off period is to give the body time to adjust to all the stresses it's undergone, particularly from lifting weights and working with the weight machines. You'll find during this tapering-off period that it will take a little time for you to feel comfortable playing basketball again. That is because you're literally playing in a different body! It's stronger, faster, more fit and powerful than the body you played in the season before. But gradually, as you get used to your body's newly minted strength and power, you'll discover that you're less tired on the court than ever before, you can jump higher, you're stronger and far more able to control the ball on shots, rebounds, and passes—in short, you're better prepared to take your game to new levels of proficiency and grace.

The exercises listed below are easy to do and fun once you get in the habit of doing them. With regard to free weights and strength machines (Nautilus, Universal, Cybex, etc.), I strongly urge you to seek the guidance of a qualified strength training instructor, at either your local Y or gym, before embarking on any strength program. The instructor is trained to teach the precise movements for any strength exercise and can tailor a program to your age and weight so that it emphasizes endurance and strength (desirable for basketball) rather than muscle bulk (generally undesirable for basketball).

Off-Season Conditioning

1. *Stretching routine:* approximately 30 to 45 minutes; includes stretching after long distance running. Daily.
2. *Jumping rope:* 5 to 10 minutes, Daily.
3. *Long-distance running:* start at 1 mile, work up to 3 miles.
4. *Wind sprints (40 yard dashes):* start with 4, work up to 8.
5. *Sit-ups:* start with 50, increase by 10 every 3 days.
6. *Push-ups:* start with 50, increase by 10 every 3 days.
7. *Weights and strength machines:* develop 3- or 4-day-a-week program with the aid of a qualified strength training instructor.

In-Season Conditioning

1. *Stretching routine:* approximately 15 to 30 minutes (see next section for desirable routine).
2. *Jumping rope:* 5 to 10 minutes.
3. *Long-distance running:* 1 mile daily.
4. *Wind sprints:* 5 to 10 daily.
5. *Sit-ups:* 25 to 30 daily.
6. *Push-ups:* 25 to 30 daily.
7. *Weights and strength machines:* 2 to 3 times a week.

Of course, on game days you won't be able to do the program—you'll be saving your energy for actual play. But you should not assume the rest of the time that just because you're playing or practicing basketball five days a week that your total body is staying fit. It isn't. Your upper body (arms, chest, back, shoulders, and abdomen) especially needs attention during the playing season lest all the strength and power it gained during the off-season training be lost. Also, playing basketball requires exceptional flexibility to avoid muscle tears and other injuries. That's where stretching comes in, and one thing you should—indeed *must*—do every day during the basketball season, on both game days and others, is stretch. Since my days as a pro I have become something of a fanatic about stretching—and I've noticed I'm not alone. Today it's common during a practice or pregame warm-up to see professional players sprawled on the court, going through their individual stretching routines. They know that a good series of stretches before strenuous activity guarantees loose muscles, a better tuned body, and a drastically reduced likelihood of injuries. In the next section, through the courtesy of two wonderful people, I want to show you a stretching routine that you can follow throughout your entire career.

STRETCHING

Several years ago, Bob and Jean Anderson put together an important book on stretching technique called *Stretching*. In it, they describe in clear detail the correct techniques for stretching, and also discuss how stretching 1) reduces muscle tension, 2) makes you feel more relaxed, 3) helps your coordination by allowing for freer and easier movement,

4) increases your range of motion, 5) helps you develop body awareness, and 6) greatly helps prevent injuries.

The following section on stretching for basketball is excerpted from the Andersons' book. I am grateful to them and to their publisher for permission to reprint the material here, and I hope it aids your game preparation as much as it has aided mine over the years.

How to Stretch*

"Stretching is easy to learn. But there is a right way and a wrong way to stretch. The right way is a relaxed, sustained stretch with your attention focused on the muscles being stretched. The wrong way (unfortunately practiced by many people), is to bounce up and down, or to stretch to the point of pain: these methods can actually do more harm than good.

"If you stretch correctly and regularly, you will find that every movement you make becomes easier. It will take time to loosen up tight muscles or muscle groups, but time is quickly forgotten when you start to feel good.

The Easy Stretch "When you begin a stretch, spend 10-30 seconds in the *easy stretch.* No bouncing! Go to the point where you feel a *mild tension,* and relax as you hold the stretch. The feeling of tension should subside as you hold the position. If it does not, ease off slightly and find a degree of tension that is comfortable. The easy stretch reduces muscular tightness and readies the tissues for the developmental stretch.

The Developmental Stretch. "After the easy stretch, move slightly into the *developmental stretch.* Again, no bouncing. Move a fraction of an inch further until you again feel a mild tension and hold for 10-30 seconds. Be in control. Again, the tension should diminish; if not, ease off slightly. The developmental stretch fine-tunes the muscles and increases flexibility.

Breathing. "Your breathing should be slow, rhythmical and under control. If you are bending forward to do a stretch, exhale as you bend forward and then breathe slowly as you hold the stretch. Do not hold your breath while stretching. If a stretch position inhibits your natural breathing pattern, then you are obviously not relaxed. Just ease up on the

*From *Stretching,* by Bob and Jean Anderson, Shelter Publications, Inc.

stretch so you can breathe naturally.

Counting. "At first, silently count the seconds for each stretch; this will insure that you hold the proper tension for a long enough time. After a while, you will be stretching by the way it feels, without the distraction of counting.

The Stretch Reflex. "Your muscles are protected by a mechanism called the *stretch reflex.* Any time you stretch the muscle fibers too far (either by bouncing or overstretching), a nerve reflex responds by sending a signal to the muscles to contract; this keeps the muscles from being injured. Therefore, when you stretch too far, you tighten the very muscles you are trying to stretch! (You get a similar involuntary muscle reaction when you accidentally touch something hot; before you can think about it, your body quickly moves away from the heat.)

"Holding a stretch as far as you can go or bouncing up and down strains the muscles and activates the stretch reflex. These harmful methods can cause pain, as well as physical damage due to the microscopic tearing of muscle fibers. The tearing leads to the formation of scar tissue in the muscles, with a gradual loss of elasticity. The muscles become tight and sore. How can you get enthused about daily stretching and exercise when these potentially injurious methods are used?

"Many of us were conditioned in high school to the idea of 'no gain without pain.' We learned to associate pain with physical improvement, and were taught that '. . . the more it hurts, the more you get out of it.' But don't be fooled. Stretching, when done correctly, is not painful. Learn to pay attention to your body, for pain is an indication that something is *wrong.*

"The straight line diagram represents the stretch which is possible with your muscles and their connective tissue. You will find that your flexibility will naturally increase when you stretch, first in the easy, then in the developmental phase. By regularly stretching with comfortable and painless feelings you will be able to go beyond your present limits and come closer to your personal potential."

There you have it: the Andersons' complete, no-nonsense stretching program for basketball players. As one who still uses it today, I can honestly report that it's safe, easy, fun, and, more important, it works. If you're not doing so already, you owe it to yourself and your body to incorporate stretching into your personal basketball program.

1

5 times
each direction

2

10 seconds
each side

20 seconds

30 seconds

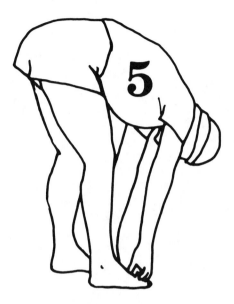

20 seconds

30 seconds

30 seconds

3 times
5 seconds each

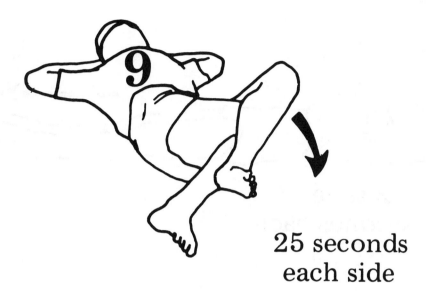

25 seconds
each side

20 seconds
each leg

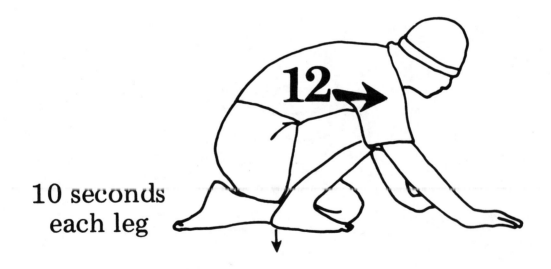

11

2 times
5 seconds each

12

10 seconds
each leg

20 seconds
each leg

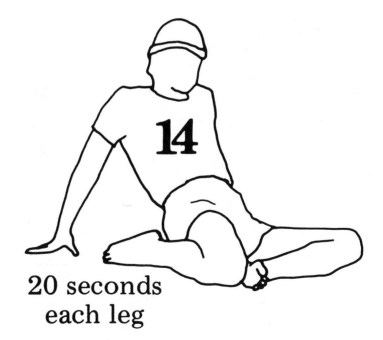

20 seconds
each leg

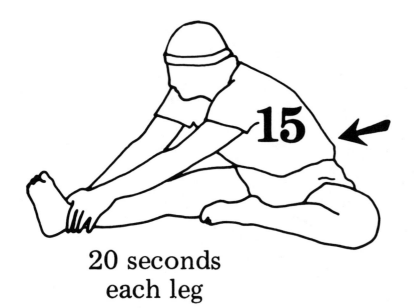

20 seconds
each leg

30 seconds

30 seconds

15 times
each direction

10 seconds
each arm

20 seconds

**30 seconds
each leg**

EATING HABITS, BODY CARE, AND MENTAL ATTITUDE

No discussion of conditioning for basketball or any other sport would be complete without mentioning the importance of proper eating habits, body care, and mental attitude. When I played professional basketball, I was appalled frankly, by the number of players whose good training habits stopped whenever it came to putting food in their mouths. Likewise, I was shocked by those players whose attitude toward the game, their coaches, their teammates, their fans and even their families smelled worse than a lockerful of old sneakers.

I propose, therefore, that you budding complete players take the following quiz to see how you compare to those professional incompletes. Consider yourself one of them if your combined score in the next three quizzes is less than nine points, but more important, start making the effort to change your negative habits now. Again, it's something you owe yourself if you really want to find out just how good a basketball player you can be.

Eating Habits

1. I overeat
   ____ Always (0 points)
   ____ Sometimes (1 point)
   ____ Never (2 points)

2. I eat greasy or fried foods
   ____ Every day (0 points)
   ____ Every other day (1 point)
   ____ Not too often (2 points)

3. I try to eat three good meals a day
   ____ Every day (2 points)
   ____ Seldom (1 point)
   ____ Never (0 points)

4. I eat foods high in carbohydrates (potatoes, pasta, etc.) and protein (beef, fish, fowl, milk, peanut butter)
   ____ Often (2 points)
   ____ Seldom (1 point)

5. I eat candy bars, potato chips, nachos, cheese puffs, ice cream, cake, brownies, cookies, soda, moon pies
   ____ Breakfast, lunch and dinner (0 points)
   ____ In moderation (2 points)
   ____ Never (I don't believe you)

6. I read the labels on food containers and try to avoid artificial preservatives, chemical additives, and excessive salt, starch, and refined sugar
   ____ Never (0 points)
   ____ Sometimes (1 point)
   ____ Frequently (2 points)
   ____ Always (5 points)

Body Care

1. I change my underwear
   ____ Never (subtract 5 points—and stay away from others)
   ____ Once a week (0 points)
   ____ Once every few days (1 point)
   ____ Every day (2 points)

2. I dress like
   ____ Conan the Barbarian (0 points)
   ____ A fashion plate (1 point)
   ____ A self-respecting player and person (2 points)

3. I expose my body to rain, cold or the sun
   ____ Excessively (0 points)
   ____ Moderately (2 points)

4. I watch my weight
   ____ Never (0 points)
   ____ When basketball season rolls around (1 point)
   ____ Throughout the year (2 points)

5. I check all injuries with the trainer or team doctor
   ____ Never (0 points)
   ____ Sometimes (1 point)
   ____ Always (2 points)

6. I shower regularly, dry well before going outside, and dry my head
   ____ Never (0 points)
   ____ Sometimes (1 point)
   ____ Always (2 points)

7. I have a physical examination at least
   ____ Once a year (2 points)
   ____ Every 2 years (1 point)
   ____ Never (0 points)

Mental Attitude

1. My outlook on life is
   ____ Pessimistic (0 points)
   ____ Mostly optimistic (1 point)
   ____ Frequently to always optimistic (2 points)

2. I respect and obey my parents
   ____ Never (0 points)
   ____ Sometimes (1 point)
   ____ Nearly always (2 points)
   ____ Always (I don't believe you)

3. I am able to live with teammates, students, fans, and coaches without conflict
   ____ Rarely (0 points)
   ____ Occasionally (1 point)
   ____ Nearly always (2 points)

4. I have conditioned myself to walk away from bad habits such as smoking, drinking, drug taking, that I know will eventually destroy my stamina and vitality
   ____ Never; I love to fill my body with poisons (subtract 5 points)
   ____ Sometimes, though I'll occasionally sneak a smoke or a hit or a drink (0 points)
   ____ I think drugs, alcohol, and tobacco are for morons (2 points)

5. I have confidence in myself, my teammates, and my coach
   ____ Never (subtract 2 points for being a negative influence)
   ____ Sometimes (1 point for honesty)
   ____ I grow more confident in my real strengths and those of my coach and teammates every day (2 points)

6. I consider myself a quality individual
   ____ Yes (2 points)
   ____ I couldn't care less what kind of individual I am (0 points)
   ____ I feel I'm trying to be (3 points for honesty)

If you score a total of 9 points or fewer, you should seriously consider taking up some other activity—like maybe trying to make yourself human again! A total score of over 9 points but under 25 indicates that there are areas in your personal life that need extra attention. See what you can do to work out those problems yourself, and if you recognize that you need extra help on a problem (though, often, just recognizing the problem itself is half the battle), then don't hesitate to go to your coach, your parents, or even a counselor or minister for guidance. So often, playing better basketball is simply a matter of correcting a bad personal habit (eating junk food, smoking, etc.) or solving a problem in the mind. Whatever your problems are (and we *all* have problems), my point is, don't let them escalate to a point where they interfere with your basketball playing ability or with any other part of your life. Take the necessary steps to get in control of yourself now.

A Few Words About Drug and Alcohol Abuse

Don't.
No matter what anybody tells you.
No matter what peer pressure is applied.
You know better.
You're finding capacities within yourself on the basketball court and elsewhere that you didn't know you had.
The D's and A's (drugs and alcohol) just diminish those capacities.
Don't.
You're too fine a person, have too many things going for you.
Remember: you're becoming a complete player.
Don't.
You're a role model to others—a role model to

yourself. Why undercut who you are and what you're doing as a player and a person with D's and A's.

They're death.

They'll come back to haunt you.

And nobody needs to go through this life haunted. Don't.

You may think you'll want to thank me later.

You'll be thanking the wrong person. Because ultimately you're the one who chooses whether or not to do drugs and alcohol. And if you choose not to do them, the only person you have to thank is yourself.

BASKETBALL INJURIES: Some Commonsense Medical Advice

No matter how carefully you play or how well you condition yourself for basketball, there still may come a day when you find yourself injured. Often players are puzzled by what to do if they're injured. After the initial panic, they wonder, "Should I stop playing? Should I apply ice or heat to the injured area?" Sometimes the trainer or team physician isn't around to answer such questions. That's why a basic understanding of appropriate immediate action can help you react intelligently if you're injured and prevent any further damage to you from occurring.

What I'd like to do now is lead you through the care and treatment of some of the most common injuries in basketball. Just because you may never have been injured before doesn't mean you should skip over this section. Despite all your efforts otherwise, you could someday be injured. It would be a shame to see your basketball career hampered forever, or even ended, because you didn't know how to treat a simple injury.

Basic Concepts of Injury Treatment

You've just twisted your knee or ankle during practice and there is immediate swelling and severe pain in the area of the injury. The trainer isn't around and your coach confesses that he doesn't remember the proper first aid. Somebody says put a hot water bottle on the injured spot. Somebody else says, no, an ice bag. You limp over to the bench, hoping somebody will give the right treatment. But which is it? Heat or ice? And how long should it be applied? And what afterwards?

If you remember what you learned in school about the human circulatory system, you'll recall that when you put your hand or foot in a bucket of hot or warm water, the heat from the water warms the blood vessels in the area, causing the area to swell, and the skin surrounding the vessels turns red. If a blood vessel is torn due to an injury, blood flows out of the torn spot, causing swelling in the surrounding area. This fact is worth noting, and many people don't realize that *swelling is caused by blood flowing into the injured area.* Therefore, it makes no sense as a first treatment to apply heat to such an injured area. By doing so, you're only causing the blood vessels in the area to swell more. More blood flows from the torn vessel into the area and the swelling (and pain) only increases.

The first-aid treatment of choice for a severe injury such as this is *ice.* The application of ice on the injury will cause the blood vessels to narrow and get smaller. That will mean less blood flowing through the torn blood vessel, causing less blood to enter the injured area, and therefore *less* swelling and pain.

Remember this fact, because someday it could save you a lot of pain and agony: For an injury where there is immediate pain and swelling, the best immediate treatment is ice. Ice treatment should continue on what doctors call an "on-to-off" basis for the first twenty-four to seventy-two hours. That means leaving an ice pack *on* the injured area until the cold itself starts to feel uncomfortable, taking it off for several minutes, putting it back on, etc., round the clock. After twenty-four hours of ice treatment the injured muscle and joints may be helped by applying heat and massage. These not only give relief to the muscles and joints, but also help speed the repair of injured ligaments, muscles, or bones.

You may have heard well-meaning people encourage an injured player to "walk it off" or "sit down a while and when you feel better, come in and play."

Because any injury causes damage—be it to ligament, tendon, muscle, or bone—these are potentially dangerous suggestions. If you're injured and the discomfort is severe and no trainer or team physician is on the scene, you've got to decide whether to play or seek medical attention. If you decide to go back into the game in which you've sprained a limb (and sprains are the most common basketball-related injuries), you must understand clearly that a sprain is a torn ligament. To continue playing with such an injury could cause that simple sprain to develop into a major ligament damage that could later require surgery. You've got to know, therefore, certain signs and symptoms likely to appear in an injured area so that you can decide whether to keep playing or not.

The Ankle

One of the most common athletic injuries to a basketball player is the "sprained ankle." The ankle joint is made up of bones held tightly together by liga-ments: tight cordlike structures that attach from bone to bone to give stability to the joint. If the ligament comes apart, doctors say that the joint "dislocates." An actual tear in any ligament is called a "sprain." It may someday happen that, coming down from a rebound or lay-up, you turn your ankle in and find that you can't bear weight on the ankle joint. You may feel a lot of pain, usually over the inside part of your ankle joint, and if you're really hurt, you'll also experience pain on the inside portion of the ankle. Swelling occurs in these painful areas. What should you do?

First, you should stop playing, go to the sidelines and apply a cold compress (an ice pack) to the sprained area. You might also gently wrap the ankle in an Ace bandage, and you should definitely keep the ankle elevated. If, after a few minutes, you're still in pain and the swelling continues, you should stop further activity—you should certainly *not* go back into the game—until a trainer or physician can see the injured ankle.

Ankle sprains generally fall into three categories:

Proper Taping Technique

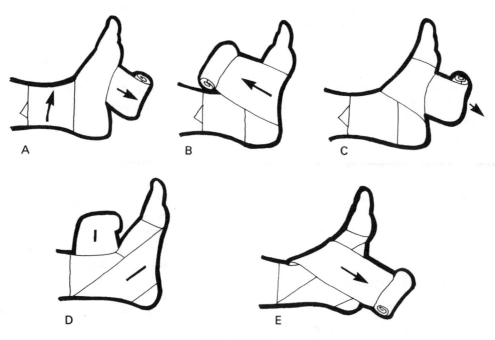

The Ankle

A **Grade I or mild sprain** occurs when a small portion of the ligament has been overstretched, resulting in small tears of the fibers that make up the ligaments. In this injury the ligament is not too badly weakened and treatment consists of applying ice and an Ace bandage until the pain decreases. It may decrease enough that the ankle can be strapped or taped, and you can resume playing. But if your ankle hurts after taping, and playing is too difficult, especially when running, turning, or twisting, you should come out of the game and a doctor should examine your ankle to determine the extent of injury. In fact, *I recommend that a doctor look at your ankle anyway, even before you go back into the game.* But sometimes a doctor isn't on the scene and that, as I said a moment ago, is when you have to make your own decision. If you keep playing, you may further damage the pulled ligament, leading to a Grade II sprain. If the Grade I sprain is treated immediately by a doctor and the ankle joint is protected during play, it should heal within four to six weeks. Though you will probably be able to play on it, the doctor will recommend rest and protection of the ankle joint in the form of a brace or bandage to give added relief to the area and encourage healing.

A **Grade II sprain** is a much more severe injury. Here, a major part of the ligament (or ligaments) is torn and playing on it will only make it worse. Usually, swelling and pain continue even after ice, Ace support, and elevation, and running and even walking hurt a lot. Grade II sprains are usually treated by immobilizing the ankle joint in a "soft cast" and in some cases a plaster cast to allow the ligaments to heal. It may take a full six weeks before you can resume your normal basketball training, and *treatment by an orthopedic surgeon specifically trained in sports medicine is a must.* Grade II sprains are not to be taken lightly. If the sprain isn't cared for properly, it will not only cause later discomfort to the injured joint, it may also progress from a Grade II to a Grade III sprain.

A **Grade III sprain** occurs when there is a complete tear of the ligament or ligaments. If your ankle is injured that severely, you'll find it impossible to bear any weight on the ankle at all, and you must resort to hopping or walking with support (crutches) so as not to place the injured foot on the ground. The ankle may feel unstable, as if it's "going out of the socket." Obviously you must stop any further activity, and the immediate attention of a doctor is essential. Grade III sprains require either surgical repair or long-term cast immobilization, depending on the findings and preferences of the doctor. It's the worst kind of sprain, a bad, bad injury that will keep you out of basketball for the rest of the season.

To repeat: You must be able to quickly assess an injury to your ankle joint if a trainer or doctor is not available. If the ankle is swollen and tender and you can't walk on it a few minutes after the injury, take yourself out of the game. Stop playing. It's for your own good. Apply an ice pack to the ankle, use an Ace bandage (compression dressing) possibly, but by all means *be sure to see a doctor as soon as possible for further evaluation and treatment.*

The Knee

The bones of the knee, like those of the ankle, are attached by many ligaments which give the knee joint its stability. It's a more complicated joint than the ankle since it not only allows upward and downward motion as the ankle does, but also rotation which enables us to turn quickly from side to side. Within the knee joint is the *meniscus*, a spongy material we nondoctors often call cartilage. The meniscus acts as a shock absorber between the thigh and the shin bones, and the most common knee injuries facing you as a basketball player are to it and to the ligaments.

Ligament injuries to the knee joint are classified just like those to the ankle joint. **The Grade I sprain** occurs when you turn too quickly or when you come down from a lay-up or rebound and the knee "gives way." In both cases a small tear in the ligament results. Pain and swelling may be immediate and you may find you are limping or favoring that leg. Time to go to the sideline and apply ice and an Ace bandage to the area. Unfortunately, unlike with a Grade I ankle sprain, a knee joint must have mobility and cannot be taped to enable you to continue. You must therefore *stop playing and seek medical attention if the pain and swelling do not subside within* *twenty-four hours.* Grade I sprains usually keep a player on the sideline for at least three weeks.

A Grade II sprain results in worse damage to the ligaments, along with more pain, swelling, and difficulty in walking. All activity should be stopped and a trained physician seen. The knee joint can be so swollen that moving the knee is excruciating. Treatment of a Grade II knee sprain may require plaster splints, casts, or knee braces, and later a program of physical therapy will help. You may be able to resume basketball in six to eight weeks if you've regained full strength and motion to the injured knee. You must, however, be able to perform your basketball skills without any pain or discomfort to the knee joint before you can consider yourself able to return to active play. Most doctors agree that you should not rely on the use of straps or a knee brace in order to resume play because a premature return to basketball can result in a long-lasting injury.

You will easily be able to detect a **Grade III sprain** because it hurts terribly, feels as if the bones in the knee joint have "jumped out of place," and standing is an impossibility. The knee joint swells immediately, and pain is felt on more than just one side of it. A Grade III sprain results in a complete tear of the supporting ligaments of the knee joint and warrants immediate attention. Before you are carried or hop off the court, the injured knee joint should be immobilized with a protective splint. If a trainer or team doctor isn't present, wrapping the knee with a shirt or towel may give some immobilization. Ice and an Ace bandage can also help, but the main thing is to have someone get you to a doctor as quickly as possible. A prolonged period of treatment is critical, and you must come to grips with the fact that you will be out for the season.

Damage to the knee joint's meniscus. Most knee injuries affect only the ligaments, but sometimes the meniscus can be damaged, too. There are actually two menisci in the knee joint; they can be injured along with the ligaments or by themselves. A twisting motion of the knee can cause the meniscus to tear; you may, as you pivot, hear a "pop" in your knee sometimes followed by a quick twinge of pain to the inside or outside of the knee joint. You may or may not lose your balance or mobility. The knee joint may or may not immediately swell. Under these conditions you *may* be able to keep playing. After the game, though, you may feel some pain in the inner or outer part of the knee joint, which might swell. You'll probably be able to walk, but the knee joint is uncomfortable. Ice, an Ace bandage, and elevating the leg may give some temporary relief, but if walking is difficult the next day and the discomfort persists, it's time to see the doctor. He or she will tell you that *you must have full use of your knee with no swelling in the joint before you can return to basketball.* If the meniscus isn't badly torn, a period of special exercise prescribed by the doctor or a physical therapist may be enough to get you on the court again. If, however, the meniscus tear is bad, then orthopedic surgery may be the only corrective step. Luckily, with today's arthroscopic surgery and intensive muscle rehabilitation programs, you may be back on the court within two to four weeks. But the length of time may be shorter or longer depending upon your individual response to the therapy program.

Muscle and Tendon Injuries of the Knee Joint

The knee can also suffer muscle and tendon injuries which most often occur when a player comes down from a rebound. If the knee happens to be severely twisted on the landing, it can give way and the player falls. When he tries to stand up he finds that his knee cannot support him. Usually what has happened is that the player has dislocated his kneecap or ruptured his knee's tendons, which attach the knee's muscles to its bones. If this ever happens to you (and I hope you're never injured in any way), you should be assisted to the sidelines where ice and an Ace (compression) bandage should be applied and the leg elevated. A doctor should be called and, needless to say, you should not plan to reenter the game. Muscle and tendon injuries usually require several weeks of treatment which includes an intensive physical therapy program. You should not return to basketball until you have regained almost *complete normal function of the knee.*

The Wrist

Sprains and ligament injuries to the wrist don't often happen since the ligaments around the wrist are numerous, and the amount of force necessary to damage them is great. Nonetheless, they can occur if you fall on your wrist or hand, and if you feel instant discomfort you should leave the game and apply ice and an Ace bandage to the injured area. If the pain isn't bad, strapping the injured wrist may allow you to continue playing. If, however, the pain is severe and dribbling and shooting hurt, you should leave the game and medical attention should be sought to be sure that the joints and bones aren't badly injured. If not properly taken care of, a broken bone (fracture) of the hand can result in permanent problems. Thus, if the wrist is badly swollen and painful, it's best to see a doctor immediately.

The Hand

Any basketball player knows that in order to dribble and shoot the ball, his hands must be in perfect condition. Finger movement must be smooth and supple, and fingertip strength must be at its maximum. If any part of the hand is hurt, performance is affected.

The most common injury to the hand occurs when the basketball hits the tips of the fingers, pushing them backward. The results may range from minor injury to the ligaments with minimal swelling and

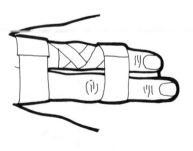

Two Fingers

pain, to dislocation of any of the joints with accompanying pain and swelling. If any part of your hand is ever injured, you should immediately apply ice to the area and evaluate the extent of the injury. If you can fully bend (flex) and straighten (extend) the finger, breathe a sigh of relief: You probably haven't dislocated or fractured it. If pain and swelling aren't severe, the team physician or trainer may decide to immobilize the injured finger by taping it to the one next to it. (This can easily be done for any finger except the thumb.) Taping the finger limits the hand's performance but does allow you to return to the game. Afterward, if swelling and discomfort persist, you should see a doctor.

If swelling and pain initially are severe, you should not return to the game but should immediately see a doctor. All too often, what appears to be a minor hand injury may actually be a fracture or severe ligament injury to its small joints. To eliminate the risk of permanent problems, the hand or fingers should be completely healed before you rejoin your team. Taping fingers together is only a temporary support measure. As long as swelling and lack of full hand mobility exist, you should not resume basketball.

The Calf and Achilles Tendon

While running up and down the court or while standing and making a quick turn, it may suddenly happen that you experience a sharp pain and "pop" in the back of your calf muscle. You find it impossible to walk or run without difficulty and have to hop or be carried off the court. There is a severe pain in the back of your calf. The most likely cause of the pain is a tear in one of the muscles of the calf which is connected to the Achilles tendon. The trainer or team physician should immediately apply ice and an Ace bandage, and further medical attention should be sought as soon as possible. If such an injury should ever happen to you—and again, here's hoping it doesn't—expect a period of immobilization on crutches followed by a rigorous program of physical therapy for six to eight weeks before you will be able to play again. If the injury involves a partial or complete tear of the Achilles tendon, then a longer period of treatment will be necessary.

Muscle Cramps

Muscle cramps, also called spasms, are a common problem for the basketball player. They can occur in almost any muscle, particularly the calf, thigh, neck, and lower back, and they're usually the result of 1) a reduction of salt in the body due to excessive sweating, 2) changes in body temperature during a game, 3) sudden overheating or chilling of the muscles during strenuous activity. Muscle cramps are not serious and you can usually treat them yourself.

When you get a muscle cramp, what's actually happened is the muscle fibers have tightened up, or as doctors say, they've "gone into spasm." The muscles neither swell nor deform, but they do feel hard or tight to the touch. If your calf muscle (located in the back of your lower leg) cramps, your foot will probably be pointing downward since the muscle in spasm has pulled on the Achilles tendon which attaches to the heel. Often you can relieve calf cramps by first gently massaging the muscle and then slowly stretching it by bringing the heel and ankle to their normal position. *Never stretch a cramped muscle fast or you're liable to tear it.*

The *hamstrings* (located in the back of the thigh) are also susceptible to cramping. If yours cramp, you may find yourself falling to the floor with your knee bent and the hamstrings tight and painful to the touch. Gently massage the muscle and then slowly try to straighten the knee so that the muscles begin to stretch.

If any muscle has cramped because it's over-fatigued, you should rest on the sidelines until all the discomfort is gone. Drink water, juices or diluted electrolytic drinks such as Gatorade to help restore body salts and prevent further spasms from occurring. *Persistent pain or discomfort may be a signal that you've torn or ruptured the muscle that's cramping,* in which case you should stop playing and seek medical attention.

The Groin

Sometimes, trying to run or maneuver quickly with the basketball, you may feel a sudden sharp twinge of pain and discomfort in the groin area. More than likely when this happens, your injury is a partial or complete tear of one of the muscles that controls movement of the hip. You will, no doubt, stop running immediately and may even fall to the ground, instinctively putting your hand over the muscle tear and drawing your knees up toward your chest to relieve the pain. Indeed, the pain may be so great that you won't be able to straighten your legs. The best first aid for such an injury is to massage the area, apply a cold compress, and then get medical attention promptly. Do not be a hero and try to keep playing: You'll just make the injury worse.

Groin pulls or tears usually heal with rest, but may require up to six weeks of inactivity. Thereafter, before going back to basketball or any other physical activity, a scheduled therapy program to rehabilitate the muscle is a must.

Blisters

Foot blisters, a basketball player's occupational hazard, are often caused by playing or practicing in new sneakers. Where skin rubs against shoe an irritation develops and a blister forms, usually on the heel or big toe. If blisters are an ongoing problem for you, check to make sure your sneakers are the proper size for your feet and break in new sneakers gradually. I always wore two pairs of dry socks when I played and sprinkled cornstarch or baby powder in my sneakers to reduce chafing. Rubbing powder or Vaseline on the feet before donning socks, I've discovered, also helps curb blisters.

If you do develop a blister on the court, stop playing as soon as possible and attend to it immediately. If the blister is small, you can probably protect it with a cut-out "donut" pad and return to the game. But if the blister is large, it may need a doctor's attention. Once it is cared for, you can usually keep playing and practicing, *but you must keep the blistered area clean to prevent infection.*

Anesthetic Injections

We've all heard stories of the athlete, injured during a game, who goes to the dressing room, receives a pain-killing (anesthetic) injection in the injured area, and returns to play. I am opposed to that practice, and many sports physicians bear me out. An athlete whose injured area is anesthetized, they say, loses that important pain signal which, in effect, tells the athlete he is hurt. If you're injured and try to resume play with the injured area numbed, nine times out of ten you'll only injure the area further. Therefore, I strongly urge you *never* to agree to a pain-killing shot for purposes of returning to a game. Nobody can force you to agree to such a shot, and nobody should try. But if someone does try to force you to take a shot to keep playing, *refuse.* It's *your body,* and it does neither you nor your team any good if you injure it further.

Closing Thoughts on Conditioning and Injuries

I hope I haven't frightened you with all this talk about injuries, but on the other hand it pays to be prepared. Don't forget that the less conditioned you are, the greater the chance of your being injured. Keep in shape, eat well, get plenty of rest, and stretch, and more than likely your basketball career will be a healthy one, free of pain and injury.

In addition, though, you should be alert to the normal hazards you potentially face when you step on the court to play or practice. Wet spots on the floor owing to leaks or player perspiration, poorly padded walls or basket supports and sideline seating—these and other hazards raise the risk of injury to the unsuspecting player. *Always play alert.* Be watchful for on-court hazards and try to avoid collisions with teammates and opponents alike. Of course, though you may be scrappy on the court, I assume you're a clean player, one who never resorts to illegal or unsportsmanlike conduct to sway the outcome of a game. There's no room in basketball for dirty play. Aside from tarnishing the game, the dirty player runs the very real risk of legal action against him if he intentionally injures another player. Play clean. Your example will rub off on everyone around you.

9

**Closing
Thoughts**

I'm not one who usually enjoys looking backward, but I do think it would be useful here to pause and consider what we've learned in the course of the last eight chapters. After reading this book, absorbing its information, and practicing the many skills and drills it presents, you should have a pretty clear picture in your mind of what you must be able to do in order to consider yourself a complete player. To begin with, you should be able to accurately shoot ten different shots (eleven if you count the dunk) with either hand, and your foul-shooting percentage should be 75 percent or better. You should be able to execute a variety of situation passes well, and your dribbling, faking, and rebounding skills should be so ingrained within you that they are now a matter of simple reflex. On offense, you should know not only the responsibilities of your own position, but those of the other positions as well. You should be able to mesh your offensive capabilities with those of your teammates, and, as a unit, the five of you should be able to perform certain basic offensive maneuvers—the pick and roll, the two- and three-man fast break, the screen, the feed pass, the in-bounding plays, and others—as if you've been playing together for years. Perhaps, too, your coach is working with you and your team on the more sophisticated offensive plays and alignments—going back door, playing the structured and less structured offensive games; if so, you should now understand how, if everyone on the team perfects his offensive role and plays alert, those alignments can crack even the peskiest defenses and result in your team scoring at will. On defense, you now know how hungry you must be in order to guard your man well. You've got the defensive stance down cold; you know how to stay with your man, how to hound him; you know about concentrating on the ball when your man's got it; and you know how to switch men, help your teammates on defense, double-team, block shots, box out on rebounds, read various defensive formations. You know quite a lot!

Most important, you know the value of proper conditioning, nutrition, stretching, and mental attitude in order to carry your game to the heights of which it is capable. Of these, proper mental attitude is, by far, the most necessary—and for some players, the most elusive attribute. Not surprisingly, there are players at all levels who shine in practice, and yet, when it comes to actual play, can't seem to put their game together. Maybe out of shyness or fear of failure, they tense and "choke"; their skills desert them and their tentativeness affects the play of everyone else on the team. These players can't seem to translate what they know into meaningful action. If you're one of them, if you freeze in real competition, don't despair. Instead, relax out there on the court; you're probably being too intense. After all, exciting as basketball is to play and watch, it's also still just a game.

If you go out on the court with the nervous belief that you can't do anything right, you probably won't. The mind has a way of fulfilling its own prophecy. On the other hand, if you say to yourself that you're just going out there and do your best and have fun—albeit intense fun—then more than likely all the facets of your game will fall into place: you'll remember what you've learned from practice, you'll try what you've drilled your muscles to do, you'll take shots, make passes . . . you'll start to trust the abilities you know are inside you.

There will be moments as you play when you will feel that you can do anything and you will be successful at it. You will know before you even leave your feet to take a one-handed jump shot that it will go in; you will know that you can steal the ball from your opponent without fouling him; you will know that you can dribble through the opposition's full-court press; you will know that you can feed a pass to your open teammate and he will score. It's a wonderful feeling, one of the great natural highs, and if you asked any pro player to tell you why he plays the game, he'd ultimately respond that it's not just for the money, but for those moments when he's playing the game to his own perfection.

But lest you think these moments happen all by themselves, they don't. You're the person who can bring his game to perfection at any time. It takes a lot of practice, a lot of grounding in the basics, but once you have those fundamentals under your belt, you can do it. How? By going out there on the court and saying to yourself that you're going to concentrate on playing your very best. You're going to play the best offense you know how, you're going to play the best defense. You're going to play as hard and as fiercely as you can for as long as you can, and *you're not going to let down, not for one second!*

The fact is, of course, that after a certain amount of time, you will let down. Few players can play to their maximum for the entire length of the game. Notice how long you *can* go to your fullest, however, before your concentration slips and fatigue sets in. Was it five minutes? Ten? Good. Now keep at it. Keep at it every game. See how long you can go before you have to take a mental break. After a while you'll discover that you're playing to your fullest for longer and longer periods of time. And one day—and

that day will come—*you'll discover that you can hold all that intensity, make it work for you, and play to perfection for an entire game.*

This is a very personal experience, and nobody can teach you the love and caring required to have it; you have to develop those feelings on your own. But if you love the game and love yourself, and care about the game and the way you play it, your efforts will be rewarded in an attitude, a sense of self and the self's possibilities that will stay with you and carry through in everything you do in life.

STAYING INVOLVED

Basketball is a game for opportunists, and the complete player is one who recognizes the opportunities available to him for improving and understanding his game. Even when he is watching basketball—in the schoolyard, the gym, the arena, on television—he makes it a point to study, absorb, and learn.

You can do that, too. When watching a basketball game in person, try to follow not only the ball, but the movement of the players as they carry out their individual assignments. Who seems to loaf on defense? Who seems to be effective? Why? Who plays selfish offense? Who plays as if he's on a team? Which style is more effective for the game being played? Why? What would you do differently out there if you were the center? the point guard? the forward? the coach?

Don't stop there. What kind of defense is each team using? Is it working? Why or why not? What kind of offense is the opposition throwing at it? Is that the best offense for cracking that defensive set?

These are just some of the questions you can and should ask yourself when watching *any* basketball game. Some of the most valuable moments for me as a young player came when I was waiting my turn to play in pickup games on the court near my high school in Hardinsburg, Kentucky. I remember making myself watch every player on that court, and in my mind, measuring myself against him, both offensively and defensively. Who would give me the most trouble if I went up for a shot, I asked myself? Who was the toughest to guard, and how tough would *I* have to play if called upon to guard him? That effort, not only at keeping my head in the game, but trying to learn by what I was watching, helped me improve as a player, and I guarantee that if you watch basketball with a clear and careful eye, you can improve as a player, too. Never watch a basketball game just for the fun of it; always try to find the insights that can help you understand the game better.

Watching Basketball on Television

For a number of years since retiring as a pro, I've been a basketball commentator on television, responsible for explaining to the viewing audience what's happening down on the floor. During my first few broadcasts I was quickly reminded that the home audience lacks the advantage of seeing the entire court, and that, therefore, I had to tailor my commentary to what they actually saw. I now do that, and I've learned in general that my understanding of the game, particularly its strategy and tactics, is enhanced by talking about it as I watch.

You, too, can improve your understanding of the game by talking about what you see. The next time you watch basketball on television, try this little exercise: Besides watching offensive and defensive off-the-ball movement and individual play as you normally would, make yourself verbalize something about the game once every minute. Your remarks may be very simple at first: "Jones is dogging it." "The entire Knicks team looks cold." But after a while, you'll find yourself noticing finer and finer qualities in what you observe. "That was a perfect pick-and-roll." "The Lakers are doing a beautiful job of collapsing under the boards and boxing out." "They ought to start feeding the ball to Parish. He's open." Etc. I call this the Instant Commentator exercise, and it's a great way to apply what you've learned in this book and elsewhere so that your eye for all the nuances of the game becomes sharper and sharper. The complete player knows that what he wants to develop in himself by watching basketball on TV or in person is *total basketball vision*. Playing Instant Commentator develops that vision, which carries over into your actual play.

SUMMER BASKETBALL CAMPS

I'm a great believer in young players attending summer basketball camps once they feel committed to the game in the ways I've outlined in this book. There are camps for every age and level of player, the fees usually aren't too high ($150 to $300 a week), and the value of constant play under quality coaching supervision is tremendous. The tricky business, if you and your family decide that basketball camp is for you, is finding the right one for your individual needs. Luckily, there are criteria for judging camps, and you should apply the following ones before you and your family plunk down any hard-earned cash.

First, *what is the purpose of the camp?* Is it really a basketball camp, or is basketball only one of many activities? These latter camps are fine if you want a total camping experience—hiking, canoeing, swimming, etc.—but if your purpose is to learn more about basketball, you may be disappointed by them. If the camp does specialize in basketball, find out all you can about the camp's teaching philosophy. Does it really teach offense and defense to campers? Do they learn the rules of the game? Most important, how much playing time is the average camper likely to see? Again, you can avoid a lot of disappointment and frustration if you ask these questions from the start.

Second, *what kinds of features and facilities does the camp offer?* Is there personal tutoring for the campers? A staff physician, certified trainer, or camp nurse in case of illness or injury? Is there a well-equipped training room? strength equipment? video taping? Are there both outdoor *and* indoor courts so that if it rains you're not losing valuable playing time? Are campers grouped merely by age, or by ability (this can make a *big* difference in your camping experience if everyone in your group is a better—or worse—player than you)? If the camp is run by a pro player or coach, will that person actually be at the camp throughout your stay? If not, how much of the time will he be there? Do guest instructors come to the camp? Who, and how often? Will the camp grow with you from year to year as your playing ability progresses? The best camps are those in which you can evolve from one year to the next.

Third, *how much does it cost?* Is there a nonre-

fundable deposit? When is the balance due? Make sure that the tuition cost includes insurance for the camper; you want to know you're insured against injury before you're injured; after may be too late.

Fourth, *where is the camp located?* Can you commute to it? Day camps are usually less expensive than resident camps. Are the camp's basketball facilities totally available to the campers, or do they have to share court time with nonbasketball groups?

Fifth, *what are meals and housing at the camp like?* Camp food may not be as tasty as Mom's home cooking, but it should be nutritious, prepared by a trained dietitian, and there should be plenty available for seconds and thirds. The housing may be spartan—cabins or even tents—but there should be adequate toilet facilities with running water and hot water for showers after practice. Although the camp provides three meals a day, it should also have a camp store where campers can buy extra juice and snacks, and a camp safe or bank where campers' money and valuables can be stored.

Make sure the camp sends you a schedule of activities for the time you'll be attending so that you'll have some idea of what your days there will be like. When packing for camp, be sure to pack extra socks, athletic supporters, soap, toothpaste, shorts, T-shirts, and towels so that you don't run short. And during your actual stay at the camp, have fun, make new friends, and don't get homesick—you'll be home soon enough! Above all, work hard on your fundamentals and let that hard work carry over into the fall basketball season.

TO PLAYER, COACH, AND PARENT: The Name of the Game Is *Communication*

Practicing and watching basketball, developing the right mental attitude, and attending a summer basketball camp can all help you toward your goal of becoming a complete player. But there is one component you should not overlook in your quest toward player completeness, and that's your relationship with your coach and parents. What I have to say on this subject of the player-parent-coach relationship is for their consumption as well as your

own, so if you can, ask your parents and coach to read the following pages, and you read them too, and think about what you can do to keep that relationship strong.

Having experienced all three roles in my life, I can say that, at best, communication between player, coach, and parent is a fragile thing, subject to all manner of breakdown. And yet, without it, I've learned, the young player's chances of developing to his or her fullest are severely curtailed. *Communication is something that every parent, coach, and player needs to work on;* by starting with that premise, all three parties stand a greater likelihood of a positive basketball experience.

To the Parent: Three Golden Rules

I'll give them to you straight and quick because you'll know what I'm talking about, and you'll know what, precisely, you need to do.

1. *Be supportive.* During the course of his or her basketball career, your child will more than likely experience some rough times. There will be losses to face, possibly injuries to cope with; your child needs to know you're there. If you think your child knows that already, think again. It's a point that needs constant telling. Tell your child you'll be there; tell him you'll be supportive no matter what. I've met kids—and I include myself in this category—whose lives have been turned around for the good thanks to basketball and other team-sport involvement. Encourage your kids to play with all their heart, but in the course of your encouragement, don't break Golden Rule #2:

2. *Don't pressure your child.* Self-explanatory, goes hand-in-hand with Rule # 3:

3. *Don't live vicariously through your child.* Just because you may never have made it as a basketball player doesn't mean your child has to reach your goal for you. Believe me, the moment you put undue pressure on your child, you risk destroying any real chances he has for discovering his own abilities and reaching his own potential. Lay off the pressure and sit back and marvel at the person you helped bring into this world.

To the Coach: The One Point You Must Never Forget

By your actions, your example and your advice, you are shaping the player's future. What happens to a player after he or she leaves basketball is just as important as his or her playing career. Therefore, no matter what amateur level of basketball you coach—recreation league, junior high, high school, or college—you must stress to your players the importance of a good education. Sports today are big business, and many coaches' jobs depend on winning, but there is absolutely no excuse for sacrificing a player's educational interests for the sake of "winning at all costs." Furthermore, even though a player may be an extraordinary athlete, it's a tragic mistake to advise him to neglect his college education in the hopes of landing a pro contract. The statistics are far too discouraging. Of every 200,000 schoolboy athletes, only one ever makes an NBA roster, and of those who play in the NBA, only a handful can legitimately be called superstars. The rest are journeymen players whose average lifespan in the pros is four years. After that, they're out of a job. Without an education, what do these players have to fall back on?

No, as a coach, you owe it to every one of your players to stress books before hoops. That means there can be no academic double standards on your team; the same standards must apply to every player. If a player can't live up to an established academic guideline, he must be suspended or cut from the team until such time as his grades improve. Painful as it may be to you as coach, there can be no waffling on this point. Every player should know his academic responsibilities, and you, as coach, must make sure those responsibilities are met. Beyond striving for academic excellence, honesty, sincerity, respect for one another, desire, and a willingness to work hard are the ingredients of a successful player-coach relationship.

I can tell you from experience there is no sweeter reward to a coach than when a player returns to him years later and tells him that he, the coach, was one of the reasons for the player's post-basketball success.

To You, the Player: Keep It in Perspective

If, thanks to all your dedication, hard work, and talent you become a Division 1-caliber high school player, congratulations—but watch out! If you're that good, college recruiters and coaches will be knocking down your door to talk to you; you'll be offered the sun, the moon, the stars just to sign a letter of intent to play at ol' State U.

Well, not so fast. The promises are fine, but you must try to read between the recruiters' and coaches' lines and see what is truly being said. We have all read too many stories about players who have graduated from college and cannot even read or write. These players were shamelessly used! You can be used, too, unless you remind yourself that *your first purpose as a student, in high school and then in college, is to obtain a quality education.* Athletic ability is not—I repeat—is not a passport to success. Your only insurance policy, the one you should take seriously from the moment you start in high school, is a sound education. No other form of "insurance" will do.

If you're uncertain about where to go to college, if you feel unduly pressured by college basketball recruiters, seek the guidance of your coach, parents, and school counselor. Even if you are not college basketball material, your coach should be doing everything in his power to make sure you have a shot at college, junior college, or vocational education. Your school counselor, too, is trained to help you clarify your goals. Seek them out. You don't want to be out in the cold, emptyhanded, when your playing days are over. Get an education. Go for the best you can. Weigh all the pros and cons of every school you consider, and don't settle for second best, no matter what any recruiter tells you.

I'm more proud of my college degree from the University of Louisville than I am of my NBA world championship ring and all the memories associated with it. You can have that pride, too, but you must understand, when all is said and done, that *the complete player is the educated player,* and everything you learn on the court is applicable in making that education real.

Play clean. Play hard. Play well. God bless you.

Appendix Basketball Camps

The following is a partial listing of the basketball camps available in the United States. Check other camp listings in the *New York Times Magazine*, in coaches' magazines, and the Yellow Pages, and apply the criteria listed on pages 134–35 to any camp you consider.

Nolan Richardson
University of Arkansas
Broyles Athletic Complex
Fayetteville, AR 72701
(501) 575-4555

Denny Crum
University of Louisville
Louisville, KY 40292
(502) 852-6651

John Thompson
Georgetown University
3700 O Street NW
Washington, D.C. 20057-1956
(202) 687-2492

Mike Jarvis
George Washington University
600 22nd Street NW
Washington, D.C. 20052
(202) 944-6651

Bobby Knight
Indiana University
Athletic Dept. Assembly Hall
Bloomington, IN 47405
(812) 855-2238

Rick Pitino
University of Kentucky
Memorial Coliseum
Lexington, KY 40506-0019
(606) 257-1916

Clem Haskins
University of Minnesota
516 15th Avenue SE
Minneapolis, MN 55455
(612) 625-3085

Dean Smith
North Carolina University
Chapel Hill, NC 27514
(919) 962-1155

Roy Williams
Kansas University
Allen Fieldhouse
Lawrence, KS 66045-8881
(913) 864-3056

Mike Glenn Foundation
3166 Big Spring Court
Decatur, GA 30034
(for deaf players only)

Pat Kennedy
Florida State University
P.O. Box 2196
Tallahassee, FL 32316
(904) 644-1461

Mike Krzyzewski
Duke University
Cameron Indoor Stadium
Durham, NC 27708
(919) 684-3777

Jim Boehelm
Syracuse University
Manley Field House
Syracuse, NY 13244-5020
(315) 443-2082

Randy Ayers
Ohio State University
410 Woody Hayes Drive
Columbus, OH 43210
(614) 292-0505

Gene Keady
Purdue University
West Lafayette, IN 47907
(317) 494-3214

Pete Gillen
Providence College
River Avenue
Providence, RI 02918
(401) 865-2266

Charles "Lefty" Driesell
James Madison University
South Main Street
Harrisonburg, VA 22807
(703) 568-6462

Oliver Purnell
University of Dayton
300 College Park
Dayton, OH 45469-1220
(513) 229-4421

Jeff Jones
University of Virginia
P.O. Box 3785,
University Hall
Charlotteville, VA 22903
(804) 982-5400

Tubby Smith
University of Tulsa
600 South College
Tulsa, OK 74104
(918) 631-3132

John Chaney
Temple University
McGonigle Hall
Philadelphia, PA 19122
(215) 204-7443

Tom Penders
University of Texas
P.O. Box 7399
Austin, TX 78712-7399
(512) 471-5093

Jim Harrick
University of California—
Los Angeles
405 Hilgard Avenue
Los Angeles, CA 90024
(310) 825-8699

George Raveling
University of Southern
California
University Park
Los Angeles, CA 90089-0602
(213) 740-8444

Todd Bozeman
University of California
Berkeley, CA 94720
(510) 612-0361

Rodney Baker
University of California—
Irvine
Irvine, CA 92717
(714) 856-6840

Dave Adam
Wake Forest University
P.O. Box 7265
Winston-Salem, NC 27109
(910) 759-5622

Perry Clark
Tulane University
James Wilson Jr. Center for
Intercollegiate Athletics
New Orleans, LA 70118-5681
(504) 865-5505

Jeff Mullins
University of North Carolina—
Charlotte
Athletic Dept., Highway 49
Charlotte, NC 29223
(704) 547-4937

Bob Huggins
University of Cincinnati
Cincinnati, OH 45221-0021
(513) 556-5847

Glossary: Common Basketball Terms

Air Ball: A shot that does not touch the rim or backboard.

Arc: The trajectory of the ball in flight to the basket.

Assist: A pass or hand-off leading directly to a basket by a teammate.

Backboard: The surface to which the basket is affixed (often glass) and also used to carom shots into the basket.

Backcourt: The half of the court away from the basket under attack.

Basket: The iron hoop through which goals are scored; a field goal is worth two points.

Blocking: A foul by a defensive player who blocks the legal path of an offensive player.

Blocking Out: Keeping your opponent away from the basket in a rebounding situation; also known as boxing out.

Brick: A shot that hits the rim or backboard hard.

Charging: A foul by an offensive player who runs into a defensive player who has legal position.

Cheap Basket: A goal scored by poor defense rather than good offensive play; sometimes called garbage baskets.

Court Balance: In an offensive set making sure there are two players back for defense when the shot is taken; also applies to fastbreak situations.

Court Sense: Being aware of everything that is happening on the court and the game situations at all times.

Double Teaming: Two defensive players guarding an offensive player who has the ball; the objective is to prevent a shot, pass, or dribble.

Dribble: A continuous bouncing of the ball, the only legal means of moving with the ball.

English: A type of spin put on the ball which can help to soften a shot while shooting.

Fastbreak: A style of offense in which a team attempts to score before the defense gets a chance to set up by running downcourt as soon as the offense gains possession of the ball.

Follow-Through: The breaking down action of a player's wrist after he has released the ball on a jumpshot or other shots; follow-through is also important in passing to help get the ball directly to the receiver.

Foul Shot: An unobstructed shot from the foul line; it is worth one point; awarded as a penalty for a foul by the opposing team.

Free-Throw Lane: The area on the floor bounded by the free-throw line; the end line under the basket, and two connecting lines forming a twelve foot lane; also called the paint.

141

Front Court: The half of the court in which a basket is under attack.

Goal-Tending: Illegal interference with a shot above the imaginary cylinder over the rim of the basket or when the ball is in its downward flight; it can be an offensive or a defensive infraction.

Hook Shot: A sweeping, one-handed field goal attempt, with the shooter's back at least partially to the basket.

Hoop: The rim of the basket; synonym for basket in the sense of a score.

Jump Ball: The means of putting the ball into play by having an official toss it upward between two players.

Jump Shot: A field goal attempt in which the ball is released at the top of a vertical jump by a player.

Lay-Up: A shot made from any of several angles alongside the basket, using the backboard as a guide.

Man-to-Man Defense: A style of team defense in which each player is assigned a specific opponent to guard anywhere on the court.

Midline: The center line that separates the front court from the back court; also known as the ten-seconds line.

Offensive Foul: A personal foul committed by a member of the offensive team; usually not involving a free throw as a part of the penalty.

Pick: A legal method of providing shooting room for a teammate by taking a position that picks or blocks a defensive player.

Pivot: Position taken by a player with his back to the basket, at the top of the free throw lane or alongside the free throw lane; also known as the post position.

Press: A style of defense in which offensive players are closely guarded and harried. Full-court press is applied all over the court; half-court press is applied only after the ball is brought across the mid-court line.

Rebound: A shot that caroms off the basket or backboard and remains in play to be recovered by either team.

Scissors Cut: When two or more players crisscross each other's path.

Shuffle Cut: After the player has made a pass; he then moves away from the pass by cutting around a teammate who has set a pick for him.

Strongside: The side of the court where the ball is in an offensive set.

Switch: A defensive technique in which players who have man to man assignments switch responsibilities with each other as their offensive men cross paths.

Technical Foul: A foul imposed for misbehavior or for some technical rules infraction. The penalty is a free throw plus possession of the ball for the offended team.

Ten-Second Rule: The requirement that a team has to bring the ball across the mid-court line within ten seconds after gaining possession.

Three-Pointer: A field goal made by a player who is fouled in the act of shooting, plus the free throw that he makes. Also in the NBA, a field goal from beyond twenty-five feet counts for three points.

Three-Second Rule: The restriction against the offensive player taking a set position within the free-throw lane or paint for more than three seconds.

Transition: Part of a team's running game where the team goes from offense to defense or vice versa.

Traveling: Illegally moving the ball by violating the dribbling rules.

Violation: Any infraction not classified as a foul. The penalty is loss of possession of the ball.

Weakside: The side of the court away from the ball in an offensive set.

Wings: Players who are running the outside lanes in the fastbreak situation or transition game.

Zone: A style of team defense in which each player is assigned to guard a designated floor area, rather than a specific player or opponent.

Index